Climbing Plants

Pandora jasminoides

KEW GARDENING GUIDES

Climbing Plants

Jane Taylor

Series editor John Simmons
OBE, VMH

TIMBER PRESS
Portland, Oregon

Front cover photograph: John Glover
Back cover photograph: Photos Horticultural

First published in 1987 by Collingridge Books,
Collingridge is an imprint of Octopus Illustrated Publishing
Michelin House, 81 Fulham Road, London SW3 6RB, England
part of Reed International Books,
in association with the Royal Botanic Gardens, Kew

First published in North America in 1992 by
Timber Press, Inc.
9999 S.W. Wilshire, Suite 124
Portland, Oregon 97225, USA.

Reprinted 1993
ISBN 0-88192-221-8
Filmset in England by Vision Typesetting, Manchester
in 11 on 12 pt Bembo

Produced by Mandarin Offset
Printed and bound in China

Contents

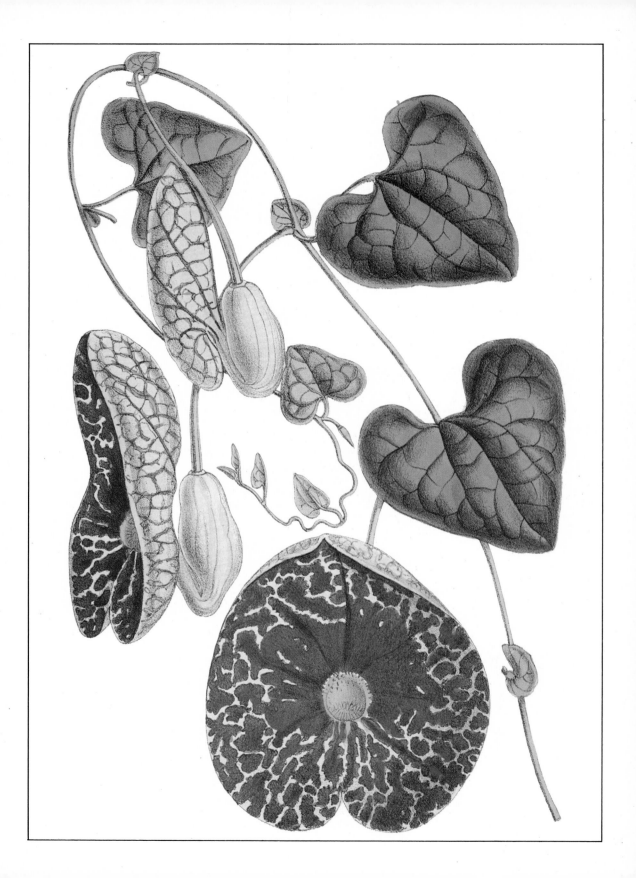

Preface

The Royal Botanic Gardens, Kew with their herbarium, library, laboratories and unrivalled collection of living plants, form one of the world's most important centres of botanical science. Their origins, however, can be traced back to a modest nine-acre site in the Pleasure Garden at Kew which Augusta, the Dowager Princess of Wales and mother of King George III, set aside for the cultivation of new and interesting plants.

On this site were grown many of the exotic species which reached England for the first time during this period of mercantile and colonial expansion. Trees such as our oldest specimens of *Sophora japonica* from China and *Robinia pseudoacacia* from America were planted for the Princess and still flourish at Kew, as do many accessions from Africa and Australia.

Many of Kew's earliest collectors were botanical explorers who made difficult and dangerous journeys to remote and unknown parts of the world in their search for economically important or beautiful plants. The work of Kew's botanists in gathering new species was complemented by that of Kew's gardeners, who were responsible for their care and propagation. The gardeners were also responsible for trans-shipping living plants from Kew to other parts of the world, and the Gardens rapidly became a clearing house through which 'useful' species grown in one continent were transferred to another.

At the present time, the living collections of the Royal Botanic Gardens contain approximately 50,000 types of flowering plants from every corner of the earth. Such a collection makes unending demands on the skills and dedication of those entrusted with its care. It also provides an unrivalled opportunity for gardening staff to familiarize themselves with the diverse requirements of plants from the many different climatic and geological regions of the world. The plants in the Royal Botanic Gardens are no museum collection, however. As in the eighteenth and nineteenth centuries, the Gardens continue to distribute living plant material on a worldwide basis, though they now use modern facilities such as the micropropagation unit at Kew and the Seed Bank at Wakehurst Place. The Gardens are also actively involved in the conservation of the world's plant resources and in supplying scientists at Kew and elsewhere with the plants and plant material required for their research. This may range from basic studies of the ways in which plants have evolved to the isolation of plant chemicals of potential use in agriculture and medicine. Whatever the purpose of the research, there is inevitably a need to grow plants and to grow them well, whether they be plants from the rain forests of the Amazon or from the deserts of Africa.

Your interest in gardening may be neither scientific nor economic, but I believe that the expert advice provided by specialist authors in this new series of *Kew Gardening Guides* will provide help of a quality that can be given only by gardeners with long experience of the art and science of cultivating a particular group of plants.

E. Arthur Bell
Director, Royal Botanic Gardens, Kew

Opposite:
Aristolochia elegans
as depicted in
Curtis's *Botanical
Magazine*, plate
6909 (1886)

Foreword

Gardening is in part instinctive, in part experience. Look in any village or town and you will see many gardens, balconies or even windowsills full of healthy plants brightening up the streets. However, there are always likely to be other plots that are sterile and devoid of plants, or overgrown and unloved. Admittedly gardening is laborious, but the hours spent sweating behind a mower on a hot summer's day will be amply rewarded when the smooth green lawn is admired; the painful nettle stings incurred while clearing ground will soon be forgotten when the buds of newly planted shrubs burst forth in spring.

These few examples of the joy and pain of gardening are all part of its attraction to its devotees. The successful gardeners and plant lovers of this world come to understand plants instinctively, learning their likes and dislikes, their lifespan and ultimate size, recognizing and correcting ailments before they become serious. They work with the seasons of the year, not against them; they think ahead, driven by caring, being aware of when conditions are right for planting, mowing or harvesting and, perhaps most important of all, they know when to leave well alone.

This understanding of the natural order cannot be learned overnight. It is a continuous two-way process that lasts a lifetime. In creating a garden, past masters such as Humphry Repton in the eighteenth century or Gertrude Jekyll in the nineteenth perceived and enhanced the natural advantages of a site, and Jekyll in particular was an acute observer of the countryside and its seasons. Seeing a plant in its natural situation gives knowledge of its needs in cultivation. And then, once design and planting have formed a garden, the process reverses as the garden becomes the inspiration for learning about the natural world.

With the widespread loss of the world's natural habitats now causing the daily extinction of species, botanic gardens and other specialist gardens are becoming as arks, holding irreplaceable collections. Thus gardens are increasingly cooperating to form networks which can retain as great a diversity of plants as possible. More than ever gardens can offer a refuge for our beleaguered flora and fauna and, whether a garden be great or small, formal or natural, this need should underpin its enduring qualities of peace and harmony – the challenge of the creative unison of formal and natural areas.

The authors of these volumes have all become acknowledged specialists in particular aspects of gardening and their texts draw on their experience and impart the vitality that sustains their own enthusiasm and dedication. It is hoped, therefore, that these *Kew Gardening Guides* will be the means of sharing their hard-earned knowledge and understanding with a wider audience.

Like a many faceted gemstone, horticulture has many sides, each with its own devotees, but plants are the common link, and they define this series of horticultural books and the work of Kew itself.

John Simmons
Editor

Introduction

It has been suggested that climbers have something of the appeal of the jungle – all those lianas and leafy creepers filled with gibbering creatures. It is a nice idea, but does not really stand up to a scrutiny of the way climbers are actually grown; in all too many gardens they are rigidly disciplined to a wall or fence, however inappropriate to their character such formal treatment might be. As we shall see, most climbers in the wild use their less supple and less opportunistic neighbours, adjacent shrubs and trees, as supports to reach for light and air, insinuating themselves among their hosts' rigid branches, twining and coiling and hooking their way to the sun, or fixing themselves, like ivy, by tenacious aerial roots. Comparatively few climbers are so highly bred, so essentially manmade, as to look at home solely in a formal setting or formally trained. Among them we may include large flowered climbing roses of the hybrid tea type and, less convincingly, perhaps the large flowered clematis.

Another image is one that assorts with the enduring fashion for cottage gardens – honeysuckle or jasmine on the porch in a fragrant tangle, adorning a cob-walled cottage beneath a thatched roof.

There are, of course, many more ways of growing climbers than these stereotypes; even a small garden can accommodate many more climbing plants than are commonly grown.

First, perhaps, the word 'climbers' as it is used in this book should be defined. With few exceptions the word is taken to mean a plant that needs some form of support if it is not to flop about on the ground. Most of these plants have evolved means of attaching themselves to their hosts or their supports; some are scramblers rather than true climbers; and a few are more properly described as trailing plants, though for lack of space most trailers have been excluded, only a few finding their way into these pages, and for entirely subjective reasons. Many climbers, deliberately planted without any support, may behave like trailing plants, or even provide effective ground cover.

This book includes a chapter on climbers in the greenhouse or conservatory; in the alphabetical section descriptions are given of many climbers that are native to warm climates and need protection from frost if grown in most parts of Europe. Tropical climbers, needing stove conditions, are excluded, however, even though several are familiar house or office plants – *Monstera deliciosa*, the Swiss cheese plant, is one. The subject of plants suitable for centrally heated offices is a highly specialized one and beyond the scope of these pages, but a few plants that are familiar in cold climates as house plants have insinuated themselves into the plant lists.

Wall shrubs are not included here. These are woody plants that are in no sense climbers, but that may be persuaded to survive in climates colder than those of their native habitats by giving them the shelter of a wall. Some of the books referred to in the list of books in the Bibliography (see page 121) describe such plants, and nurserymen's catalogues in particular frequently list many shrubs suitable for furnishing walls, either as a separate section or with a note or coded symbol against their names.

1
Climbing Plants in the Wild

Climbers attach themselves by several different methods. Some have twining stems, which curl around the host stems either clockwise or anticlockwise – the same way, almost always, for any given species. In others it is the leaf stalk, or tendrils derived from the leaves themselves, or from stipules, that coil round the supporting branches. Some tendrils, as in virginia creeper, have little adhesive pads at their tips. Aerial roots adhere even more tenaciously to their supports, as anyone who has tried to peel ivy from a host tree will testify.

By comparison with these plants that have developed coiling or self–sticking methods of hauling themselves skywards, climbers that rely on hooked prickles are often less efficient. Roses, for example, though they may get to great heights in a host plant, are never so firmly attached as a honeysuckle, say; but as their stems become more woody so they develop a firmer stemhold. Other plants that use hooks to attach themselves are those that bear their prickles on the backs of their leaves or at the leaf tips.

Plants attach themselves to their supports in various ways: (*from left to right*) cobaea by tendrils; ivy by aerial roots; honeysuckle by twining stems; roses by hooked prickles

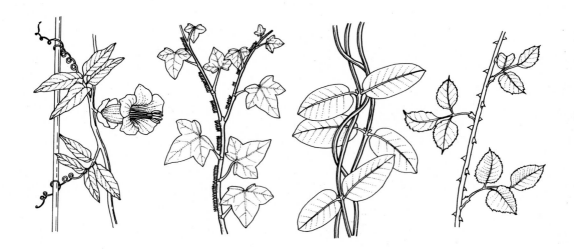

ORIGINS OF CLIMBING PLANTS

Climbing plants native to Britain are not numerous, though some are widespread and very evident – the cosmopolitan ivy most of all, perhaps, with traveller's joy or old man's beard, *Clematis vitalba*, prominent on chalk or lime soils, where it forms dense growth, the oldest stems as thick as an arm. These stems loop from support to support, attached by coiling leaf stalks, whereas common honeysuckle, *Lonicera periclymenum*, twines entire stems around host branches and may in time strangle them as its hold tightens.

Opposite: *Wisteria floribunda* and the white flowered *W. floribunda* 'Alba' (see page 113)

15

For its sweet scent, and in spite of its damaging ways, honeysuckle is a garden favourite. The same cannot be said of the bindweeds, pale pink *Convolvulus arvensis* and the larger flowered white bindweed, *Calystegia sepium*. There cannot be a gardener who has not at some time struggled to control these weeds, whose herbaceous stems twine around any support and whose white, brittle roots snap when too hastily excavated, leaving behind a scrap of tissue from which the whole superstructure will grow again in no time. Modern chemicals make bindweed easier to control, but it remains a pernicious and dreaded weed.

Neither black bryony, *Tamus communis*, nor white bryony, *Bryonia dioica*, earns a place, though the former in particular can be a handsome thing in fruit in the outermost reaches of a wild or woodland garden, decking host shrubs with its lustrous, heart-shaped leaves and large, shiny red berries. Nor would the average garden be a suitable place to grow the dog rose, *Rosa canina*, which at woodland edges will behave like a climber and hook itself up into the trees. *R. arvensis* is the field rose, a scrambler with creamy flowers, described later in these pages. Yet another British and northern hemisphere native, the common hop, *Humulus lupulus*, has a handsome garden form 'Aureus', with lime-yellow foliage. The wild plant is a luxuriant climber from which selections have been made, grown in the hopyards of Kent and Herefordshire, to flavour bitter beer.

The range of many of these climbers extends into Europe or even further afield, spanning much of the northern cool temperate zone. Europe boasts many honeysuckles and several delightful clematis, *C. alpina* and *C. viticella* among them, and from the Iberian peninsula *C. campaniflora*. The Mediterranean region gives us not only honeysuckles but also *Clematis cirrhosa* var. *balearica*, *Smilax aspera* and the silk vine, *Periploca graeca*. The grape vine, *Vitis vinifera*, for so long cultivated in the Mediterranean region, is believed to have originated in Asia Minor and the Caucasus.

Indeed, as we move eastwards to Asia Minor and Central Asia, the number of garden-worthy climbers increases. For example, the range of the common jasmine, *Jasminum officinale*, for so long cultivated on account of its exquisite perfume, extends eastwards of the Caucasus.

From the Himalayas come such familiar garden climbers as *Clematis montana* and the Himalayan musk rose, *Rosa brunonii*, together with less common but equally worthy plants such as the deliciously fragrant *Holboellia latifolia* and the red-fruited *Schisandra rubriflora*.

Moving further east again, China and Japan are the homes of some of our best loved garden climbers. Clematis again, honeysuckles, jasmines and roses abound in China, with *Celastrus*, *Actinidia* (in which genus is found the Chinese gooseberry), climbing members of Hydrangeaceae and Vitaceae, *Rubus* and *Schisandra* species, wisterias and *Trachelospermum* species. These last two genera also occur, together with *Clematis*, *Akebia* and much else, in Japan.

Several genera span the Pacific to occur not only in the Far East but also in North America. These include such cosmopolitan groups as the vines, honeysuckles, wisteria and clematis, and also such lesser known or less extensive genera as *Decumaria* and *Campsis*.

Moving southwards into another continent, from South America hail many of the most exciting climbers that can be grown outside in cool climates. *Berberidopsis* and *Mitraria*, *Eccremocarpus* and *Tropaeolum*, *Asteranthera* and

Lapageria, *Bomarea*, *Mutisia* and *Mandevilla* and the great passion flower family are just a few of the most spectacular.

Across the ocean in Australasia, both Australia and New Zealand have given us some fine climbers for the garden. The bluebell creeper, *Sollya*, and *Billardiera* with its deep blue fruits, are fairly hardy despite their origins. Others, especially from Australia, are very much plants for the conservatory except in very mild climates – *Kennedia* and *Hibbertia*, *Hardenbergia* and the like.

Australasia, of course, does not have a monopoly of tender climbers. Tropical and subtropical areas of the other five continents contribute their quota of exotic, often powerfully fragrant climbers needing frost protection. Gloriosas from tropical Africa can jostle, in a large enough conservatory, with *Hoya carnosa*, the wax flower with a range, in the wild, extending from southern China to northern Australia; with the morning glories from tropical America, Madeiran *Jasminum azoricum* or the South African *J. angulare* and, from the same continent, *Plumbago capensis*. Huge-flowered *Lonicera hildebrandiana* comes from Burma, and so does *Rosa gigantea*. To them we could add Brazilian *Passiflora* species and *Dipladenia*, and many of the gorgeously exotic members of the Bignonia family. Plenty of these lovely tender climbers are described in the alphabetical section that follows, enough to fill the grandest conservatory.

NATURAL HABITATS OF CLIMBING PLANTS

So much for a hurried look at the native countries of our garden and greenhouse climbers. But what of their habitats in the wild? Many climbers are plants of woodland edges, their roots in shade and their heads in the sun: their adaptation to their ecological niche has been not to evolve to a more efficient use of low levels of light, as have ground-dwelling plants that occur naturally in shaded sites, but to develop means of using their neighbours to reach the light they cannot do without. This is not to say that all climbers must have their heads in the sun; some, *Lonicera tragophylla* for one, are quite at home in complete, if not dense shade. Most ivies are also very tolerant of shade. Not all climbers grow in copses, woods or forests, or in the more artificial conditions of hedgerows; some are found on rocky cliffs, or scrambling among rocks and boulders – thus, for example, *Clematis alpina* in its native Alps, or *Schizophragma integrifolium* which is said to grow on rocky cliffs in its native China. *Clematis phlebantha*, from Nepal, apparently grows there on hot, dry cliffs.

Sooner or later, when writing about plants in the wild, one feels compelled to quote Reginald Farrer, who saw so many of them in their native lands. Listen to him on *Clematis tangutica* subsp. *obtusiuscula*, which 'unfurls a coil almost as long as its name over the river-shingles of all the streams above Jo-ni, ascending to about 10,000 feet on the fringes of the alpine coppice'. (*Royal Horticultural Society, Proceedings*, 1921.) Or on *Rosa filipes*, in western China: the 'hedges are filled with a gigantic rambler rose, which casts abroad twelve-foot slender sprays . . . which in their second season are bowed into arches by the weight . . . of huge loose bunches of snow-white blossom' (*On the Eaves of the World*).

It is all very distant, and not just in miles, from garden climbers regimented onto the walls of our neat dwelling houses.

2
Climbers in the Garden

Climbers can be woody or non-woody, evergreen or deciduous, with herbaceous stems dying back to a perennial rootstock each year, or of annual or biennial character. Many plants that are grown as annuals in cool climates, sown early in heat and hastened to flowering size in one season, are perennials in the wild in their warmer native habitats, and this is true of some climbers as much as of several familiar bedding plants. Climbers commonly grown as annuals, though in fact of perennial character, include such well-known kinds as black-eyed Susan, *Thunbergia alata*, and the cup and saucer vine, *Cobaea scandens*. Others, almost as familiar or less well known, are described in the alphabetical section.

When tempted by a climbing plant at their local nursery or garden centre, most people probably think first of available wall space. Walls certainly have a particular value in the shelter and warmth they can provide, enabling us to grow plants that would not survive, or would fail to reach their potential, in the open ground. This is, of course, just as true of climbers as of other tender plants, including the woody plants listed as wall shrubs in many nurserymen's catalogues. There are also, however, several other sites for climbing plants grown in almost every garden.

Opposite: Climbing plants can add so much interest to the garden, clothing arches, pergolas and masking unsightly sheds and walls

Left: *Cobaea scandens* 'Alba' (see page 73)

WALLS

Virtually every house – every detached house, at least – has four potentially usable walls. This is not to say that all these walls could, or even should, be covered. But those who inhabit gracious Georgian structures, or beautiful listed buildings of any other age when domestic architecture had not lost its way, are privileged in a way that is denied to most of us. All too many houses would be the better for some seemly veiling, and in this, climbers and wall plants are our willing allies. If there is no provision for plants to grow on the walls of your house because a paved or concrete path abuts the foundations, do consider ripping it out, if not entirely then at least here and there, to permit some planting.

Walls need not belong to a dwelling house, of course. Sometimes we may have an unsightly shed, or a summerhouse of more utility than beauty, that could be partly or wholly covered with climbers. Many vigorous climbers could perform the role of total concealment; or these walls, too, could be used to shelter the less hardy plants.

Supports for climbers

Methods of attachment, and which climbers to choose, will be similar for the dwelling house walls and for outhouses. One of the most satisfactory methods of fixing supports is by vine eyes, protruding 10 cm (4 in) or so away from the wall, and linked by braided wire running both horizontally and vertically to form a wide mesh. The cheaper alternative, plain galvanized wire, is more apt to sag; nails are usually a most unsatisfactory means of attachment. An alternative is a well-built wooden trellis. The panels of trellis should be treated with a non-toxic wood preservative, and may then be fixed at about 10 cm (4 in) from the wall. Plastic-covered mesh or trellis can be bought in various unconvincing greens and browns, or in white; such supports seldom look anything but inappropriate and obtrusive.

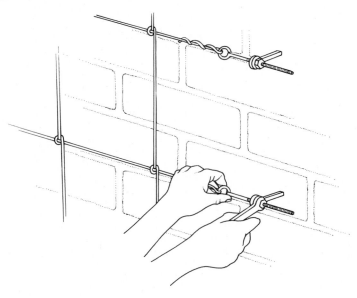

Vine eyes should be long enough to hold the wires clear of the wall

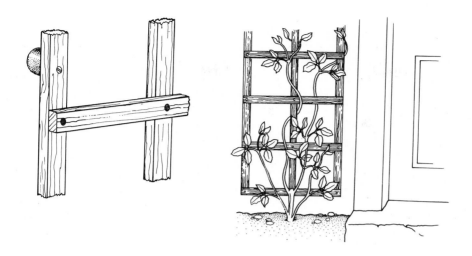

Wooden trellis can be fixed to a wall to give support to climbers. Make sure there is enough space between trellis and wall stems to allow stems to twine comfortably

Whatever the chosen means of support, it must be strong enough to take the weight of the climbers, which in time may be quite considerable. It is most distressing to find, perhaps after a night of gales and heavy rain, a treasured climber torn from its sheltering wall because its inadequate support has given way.

Choosing climbers for walls

How much or how little you decide to conceal of your walls is a matter of personal choice. It will to some extent influence your selection of climbers. Another consideration will be aspect. On north- or east-facing walls, provided they are not densely shaded by nearby buildings or trees, some roses and many *Clematis* will perform well, especially the Atragene *Clematis* – *C. alpina* and *C. macropetala* – the montanas, and many large flowered kinds. Some honeysuckles are happy in positions where there is little direct sunlight, especially *Lonicera tragophylla* and its hybrid offspring *L. × tellmanniana*. The climbing hydrangeas, *H. petiolaris*, *Schizophragma hydrangeoides* and *Pileostegia viburnoides* should do well, as should many vines, including *Parthenocissus henryana* and *Vitis coignetiae*. *Celastrus orbiculatus* also thrives without much direct sunlight, but is a plant for less formal settings than the walls of a house, as is *Berchemia racemosa*. All these except *Pileostegia* are deciduous; evergreen climbers for these positions include *Berberidopsis corallina*, *Mitraria coccinea*, *Lapageria rosea* (preferably with additional shelter from drying winds) and, of course, ivies.

Warm south- or west-facing walls can be reserved for the more tender climbers, or those that need a thorough baking in summer to induce them to flower: *Campsis* and *Passiflora caerulea*, *Solanum jasminoides*, the passion flower lookalike *Clematis florida* 'Sieboldii', grape vines (especially if you hope for fruit), *Mandevilla suaveolens*, the Banksian roses if the garden is in too cold a climate for them to be flung into some tall host tree, and much else besides. Lists of climbers suitable for various aspects are provided on page 115. As a general observation, however, twining climbers are less suitable for walls than self-stickers or those holding on by coiling tendrils.

Climbers on fences

Fences such as larch-lap or some other solid construction offer something of the same protection as walls, though retaining less heat and therefore providing less frost protection in winter. Open fences, ranch style or post-and-rail, chain-link or chestnut paling, provide another kind of opportunity to grow climbers. A screen of climbers can be supported by a fence to make what has sometimes been referred to as a 'fedge' – a word that, happily, does not seem to have caught on, though the idea it expresses could be used more. A hedge usually takes up a good deal of lateral space; a fence, unadorned, may look rather stark. But a living screen of supple climbers trained on to a suitable fence can give the visual effect of a hedge without robbing the garden of so much space. Clematis and rambler roses, vines and honeysuckles, jasmines and much else can make a fragrant and flowery screen. On the shady side of a fence ivies can be trained flat to make a uniform green or variegated barrier of foliage with all the unifying effect of a hedge within a much smaller compass.

Opposite: A pergola can support a number of different climbing plants. Here *Solanum crispum*, climbing roses and a large flowered hybrid clematis harmonize to prolong the flowering season

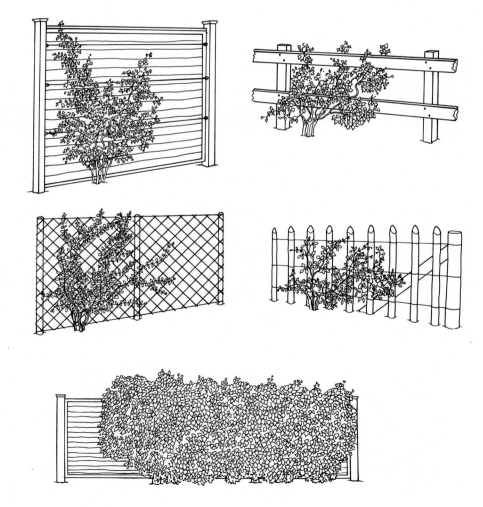

Many types of fencing make suitable supports for climbers. Unsightly fencing such as chain-link can be concealed by a dense climber which will need no other support. However training wires may be necessary for larch-lap fences. The ultimate in covering is known as a 'fedge' (bottom), for which ivy is particularly suitable

OTHER SITES FOR CLIMBERS

If only walls and fences are used to give support to climbers in the garden, their number will be needlessly restricted. Other constructions may be used, from a complex pergola to a single pole or tripod. A porch may be attached to the house that can be clothed in climbers in the same way as the house walls; or an arch can be constructed to frame a doorway and support a rose, a honeysuckle or some other climber. Free-standing in the garden, arches need to be placed carefully; too often they are rather arbitrarily set over a path to look more like an afterthought than a planned element in the design of the garden.

A pergola or a series of arches should also have a purpose, leading to a feature – a garden view, perhaps. Pergolas can be constructed from wood, or from masonry pillars with wooden crossmembers. Whatever the chosen material, they should be of solid construction; flimsy poles, whether rustic or sawn, will never be satisfactory. The material chosen should fit in with the style of the garden. The least formal will be rustic timber throughout, or stone pillars, round or square, with rough-cut beams. Brick or tile uprights with sawn timber crossmembers will give a more formal effect. The pillars can also be linked with ropes, as at Wisley or in Regent's Park. If the classic pergola with crossmembers is chosen, it should be made high enough so that even when the covering climbers, wisteria, vines or roses, are in flower or fruit, their hanging tresses clear the heads of those walking beneath.

If the pillars and the crossmembers are to be clad with plants both vigorous climbers, reaching across the width of the pergola, and smaller-growing kinds or even shrubs will be needed. Most tall climbers suitable for clothing the crossmembers will become bare at the base, and their limbs may be concealed with shorter-growing kinds that can be kept furnished to the ground. Slender climbers such as *Billardiera longiflora* or *Sollya heterophylla*, the shrubbier honeysuckles – especially *Lonicera × brownii* and its derivatives – and some *Lathyrus* would be suitable. Of rather greater vigour are the coloured-leaved *Actinidia kolomikta* or *A. polygama*, *Eccremocarpus scaber* and the clematis, though the tendency of some clematis to develop bare legs should be remembered. Pillar roses could also be chosen, especially in more formal settings. For the crossmembers it is best to choose plants with hanging flowers, or all the display will be held out of sight facing the sky.

If your garden, or your purse, cannot accommodate a pergola, there may still be scope for a more modest structure such as an arbour or a gazebo.

An arbour should be a place to sit, so fragrant plants will be especially welcome to clothe it. You may also wish to sit in your gazebo, for the dictionary defines a gazebo as a place 'whence a view may be had', giving as alternative names belvedere, turret and balcony, so your climbers should clothe it without obscuring the view. Densely leafy climbers are unlikely to be suitable.

CLIMBERS FOR SCREENING

You may wish to obscure a view, either to hide it entirely or to divide one part of the garden from another. Screens and trellis can be used for this, giving greater height than most internal hedges and taking much less ground. If you can run to an extremely decorative trellis you may well wish not to cover it too much, but if you choose a simple latticework type a few climbers to decorate it may add to its appearance. However, as a screen is likely to be of flimsy construction compared to a pergola, or even an arch, too many climbers could endanger the whole structure. Something light-limbed such as a clematis is likely to be the best choice.

Climbers can be supported by structures varying from a simple tripod or single arch to an elaborate pergola or gazebo

pergola

gazebo

pillars linked by ropes

arch

tripod

OTHER SUPPORTS FOR CLIMBERS

Pergolas, screens and gazebos, though you may erect them to provide homes for more climbers than you could otherwise find room for, are all features in their own right. Other structures, such as poles, tripods and even pyramids, are no more than supports for climbers, probably within a mixed border where height is needed without width. Many climbers can be grown on poles: roses and *Clematis*, naturally, honeysuckles and jasmines, ivies and sweet peas. Those with annual stems, or which are annually pruned almost to ground level, can have the new stems gently tied in with soft string at hand-span intervals or so. More permanent climbers such as ivies, once encouraged to grow and to adhere, should need no more than a little trimming now and then.

For more vigorous climbers, or where a more substantial feature is needed, a tripod or a pyramid can be used, its broader base giving an impression of stability. At the other extreme, for annual climbers especially or for wholly herbaceous kinds, peasticks may even be enough. I have seen *Tropaeolum tuberosum* very effectively used as a kind of suspended ground cover, attaching itself to peasticks which had been half snapped at about knee height from the ground and left horizontal; the climber quickly leafed up to hide the peasticks and held its massed orange and red nasturtiums vertically above its foliage.

Opposite: *Clematis* 'Lasurstern' clambers among the flowers of the snowball tree, *Viburnum opulus* 'Sterile'

Right: *Humulus lupulus* 'Aureus' trained up a tripod adds height and interest to a green border

CONTAINERS

Some climbers can be successfully grown in containers. The pink and blue *Clematis macropetala* in a big Ali Baba jar at Sissinghurst are famous and much copied. Urns and tubs can also hold climbers. If you wish the climber to cascade downwards from a height, like the Sissinghurst clematis, then of course a supple climber must be chosen. If you have a house with concrete footings and path that you dare not remove lest damp ruin your walls, you could as a compromise grow a variety of climbers in tubs against the walls, as long as you treat them generously.

Climbers can be grown in containers, but remember to give them adequate water and nourishment. They will also need support, either from within the container or from an adjacent wall

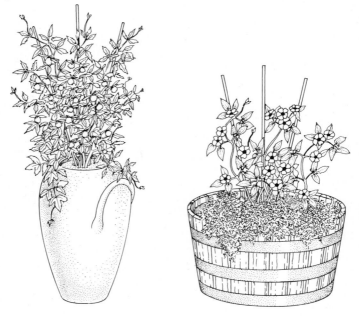

HOST PLANTS

The most natural way of displaying your climbers is in some suitable host tree, shrub or hedge. There is a wonderful photograph in an old gardening book I have showing a wisteria filling a tall oak tree, its long skeins of flowers decking the host almost from top to bottom; and the immense Kiftsgate rose, occupying two or three full-sized trees, is famous. At a more modest level, many gardens have an old, unproductive apple tree or two, or a tree of little merit except that it is hiding an ugly view. These could well act as host trees to a rose, a clematis, a honeysuckle (remembering the honeysuckle's strangling ways), a vine . . . Try, for example, a vine chosen for its autumn colour – *Vitis coignetiae*, perhaps – in a birch; the contrast of the plate-sized scarlet foliage of the vine and the golden coin-sized leaves and white bark of the birch is startlingly effective. Very leafy trees will be unsuitable, and you would scarcely wish to clutter up a rarity with a climbing companion, but many decorative garden trees have an off-season that could be enlivened with a suitable climber.

For the smaller climbers, a host shrub may be large enough as support, and the same principle applies. Alternatively, you could deliberately plant the two to coincide in flower, giving a contrast of form and colour or subtly setting two similar tones together. I have seen this done to great effect with the pink form of *Clematis macropetala* 'Markham's Pink', and chocolate-purple *Akebia quinata*, flowering together in pale and dark dusky tones in spring. This, of course, is a combination of two climbers, and later in the season roses and clematis could combine on walls or in a host tree or shrub. Once you begin to consider each shrub of reasonable size in your garden as a potential support for a climber, you may be astonished at the number of climbers you can find room for.

Hedges, too, can be hosts to a climber. The yew hedges at Hidcote, sombre setting for the brilliant scarlet *Tropaeolum speciosum*, are seen and perhaps copied by thousands of visitors each year. If your hedge is a fine feature itself, as a mature clipped yew hedge is, then such a slender-stemmed, herbaceous climber would be a wise choice, lest the hedge be damaged by a blanket of alien foliage. On rougher hedges, you can be less cautious and plant a great variety of climbers.

Your tree supports need not necessarily still be living. A tree stump, cut high and perhaps with some of its main branches shortened, not removed, could hold a climber or two of not too great vigour. Cut lower, the stump could be concealed with a sprawling climber.

From stump-hiding to growing climbers 'free-standing', to sprawl as they will, is a short step. Some climbers will make satisfactory ground cover in this way, with or without some encouraging peasticks to give them the idea of growing horizontally. Or you could copy the combination of clematis on heathers, first, I believe, tried at Burford House in Worcestershire. You need clematis that are annually pruned to near ground level, or the heathers will be ruined very quickly. The viticellas are ideal, their fairly small flowers in proportion to the hummocky heathers. Other ground-cover shrubs could act as hosts in the same way.

SCENTED CLIMBERS

So far I have considered the visual aspects of planting design with climbers. Another element in garden design, and one that is strangely overlooked, is fragrance. Perhaps this neglect is exacerbated by the high quality of colour photography today: when so many gardening books are able to rely more on vividly effective colour illustrations than on descriptions, fragrance is all the more likely to be forgotten. Indeed, it is hard enough to describe in words; unless a scent is reminiscent of some other, familiar aroma that can be used to describe it, we must fall back on the banal 'sweetly scented' or as many equivalent phrases as the thesaurus can be persuaded to yield.

With just a little extra care at the design stage our gardens can be wonderfully enriched by that extra dimension of fragrance, and climbers have much to offer. The great groups of fragrant climbers are the roses, the jasmines and the honeysuckles, and they are also among the most beautiful we can grow. Many of them share the characteristic of a perfume that is free on the air; that is, we have no need to stoop or reach to their flowers to enjoy their scent. Unequalled among roses for this generous trait are the Synstylae roses, those great, abundant, rambling species and their near allies of mixed parentage that fill the garden with swags of flower in mid summer and for a few weeks afterwards. Many of the yellow Noisette roses, too, typified by the famous old 'Gloire de Dijon', are richly perfumed. Though one does not scorn a rose that is fast of its scent, there is a particular delight in the kinds that give so freely of their fragrance.

Both jasmines and honeysuckles are more fragrant at night. It is a sad fact, to some, that the most vividly coloured honeysuckles are those without scent; but colour is not everything, and the wonderful sweet perfume more than compensates. Fragrant honeysuckles come in cream, or are flushed with warm purple-red – soft tones that blend with most other shades where the harder orange-reds of the scentless kinds may be difficult to place.

Jasmines are even more restrained in colour, though no less generous with their perfume. *Jasminum* × *stephanense* inherits from one fragrant parent its pink tones, but all others are white, though perhaps opening from red-pink buds. Some need frost protection, some are hardy; the different species flower at different times of the year so we can enjoy their almost cloying perfume over a long season.

Opposite: *Jasminum* × *stephanense* is sweetly scented and vigorous (see page 80)

Right: *Lonicera etrusca*, one of the fragrant honeysuckles (see page 85)

By contrast with the exotic jasmine scent, the fragrance of wisterias is fresh and sweet, though by no means restrained. The best scent comes from the cultivars of *Wisteria sinensis* and from *W. venusta*; in comparison the great trails of *W. floribunda* forma *macrobotrys* are only faintly perfumed.

Some clematis are fragrant; not the large flowered hybrids, but some of the species. The winter-flowering *C. cirrhosa* var. *balearica* has a lemon-fresh scent usually unnoticed as it flowers outside, but easily detectable indoors. Later, in spring, some kinds of *C. montana* are vanilla-scented, and one, the true, late-flowering *C. montana* var. *wilsonii*, is said to give off 'great wafts of hot chocolate aroma'. I should like to smell this for myself; it sounds wonderful. The vanilla scent of *C. armandii* also carries well.

In late summer *Clematis serratifolia*, a softly coloured species in the yellow-lantern group, is fragrant, and so too are the pale yellow bells, reminiscent of cowslips, of *C. rehderiana*. *C. flammula* is the southern European equivalent of Britain's native old man's beard, with masses of little white flowers, their scent likened by Christopher Lloyd to meadowsweet or hawthorn – 'a sickly kind of fragrance that yet meets you very pleasantly on the air'.

Even less showy in flower, *Holboellia latifolia* and the closely related *Stauntonia hexaphylla* are nonetheless valued for their delicious fragrance. So too are the trachelospermums, evergreen climbers with jasmine-like flowers, white or cream, in late summer. The hoya-like *Wattakaka sinensis* has a sweet, if elusive, scent, as does pink or white *Araujia sericofera*. This is one of the few hardy or near-hardy south American climbers with scent. Another is *Mandevilla suaveolens*, and yet another *Lardizabala biternata*. This is related to the Asian akebias, with sweetly scented, chocolate-purple flowers.

FLOWERS ALL YEAR ROUND

The value of climbers is not restricted to flowers, fragrant or not. Some have handsome foliage, some are noted for autumn colour or for fruit. But if flowers, above all, are what we demand from the climbing plants in our gardens, in all but the coldest climates it should be possible to have climbers in flower virtually all year.

The gardening calender begins with spring, with the renewal of the natural cycle, and at this season only a few frost-hardy climbers are in flower. *Clematis alpina*, the tough little Atragene with blue or dusky rose bells, and evergreen *C. armandii* open the season in early spring (unless you count *C. cirrhosa*, which flowers in winter). At much the same time the small, dull, beige-mauve, exotically fragrant flowers of *Holboellia latifolia* open unseen among its large leaves. By late spring many more clematis are in flower, and the first of the honeysuckles and wisterias, with the uncommon *Schisandra* species. At mid summer clematis, honeysuckle and wisteria are joined by the first of the climbing roses and several jasmines.

High summer still sees many clematis, jasmines and honeysuckles in flower, and they are joined by the climbing hydrangeas, several passion flowers, *Trachelospermum* species, and southern hemisphere climbers such as *Mutisia*, *Mitraria*, *Solanum*, *Eccremocarpus* and *Rhodochiton*. As summer advances into autumn the tropaeolums, *Berberidopsis corallina* and wax-belled *Lapageria rosea* join their southern hemisphere relatives that began their long season a month or two earlier. Campsis, too, are late summer flowers, needing all the sun they can get in cool climates. Many of the less hardy climbers that can be treated as annuals will continue to bear flowers until cut down by frost, so in mild climates they may be with us nearly until Christmas.

FOLIAGE COLOURS

Also in autumn comes the time of climbers whose dying foliage flares to crimson and scarlet and flame. All the vines, *Vitis* and *Parthenocissus* and *Ampelopsis*, give as generously as any autumn-colouring tree or shrub at this season. Some have showy fruit, such as *Celastrus*, some of the Synstylae roses, *Billardiera*, *Schisandra*, and of course some of the vines; and the shaggy seedheads of several *Clematis* are also attractive.

Some climbers provide their effect over a long season because of their handsome foliage. The vines again score well, and the ivies; there are also many climbers with variegated leaves. Ivies notably, of course, run to variegations, but there are also variegated forms of jasmine, the golden-netted honeysuckle, weak little *Ampelopsis brevipedunculata* 'Elegans' and the more acceptable variegated *Trachelospermum jasminoides*. The coloured markings on the leaves of *Actinidia kolomikta* and *A. polygama* are natural, but no less striking than some of the boldest garden forms of ivy.

There are fewer climbers with coloured foliage than there are shrubs or trees. Of grey or glaucous foliage there is not much beyond the blue-glaucous foliage of *Lonicera splendida* and the greyed leaves of the dusty miller vine or of *Araujia sericofera*. *Vitis vinifera* again gives us a purple-leaved climber in the Teinturier grape, while *Trachelospermum jasminoides* and *T. majus* often turn deep red in winter. There is a golden ivy, 'Buttercup', and a golden hop.

Let it not be thought, from the brevity of this list, that climbers have little to offer in the way of foliage. As well as the coloured-leaved and variegated kinds, and those few with bold leaves, there are many with attractive green foliage, deciduous or persistent. These, above all, are the climbers to choose for prominent positions in the garden.

3
Care of Climbing Plants

Climbers in the wild are almost invariably found growing close to other plants, which they use as a support to reach light and air. Though their roots may be in competition with the root systems of their host trees and shrubs, they also have the benefit of cool, leafy soil, shaded from direct rays of the sun and thus seldom dry and parched.

CULTIVATION

This can be our guide to soil conditions in the garden: ample humus, abundant moisture especially in the growing season, and adequate fertility. Peat and pulverized bark are often sold as soil improvers, and they do indeed add humus; but their food value is very limited, and unless garden compost or well-rotted manure can also be incorporated into the soil, or some good leafmould, fertilizers should be added with the peat or bark. Thin, sandy soils and heavy, sticky clay especially benefit from ample humus, both at the time of planting, when it can be well mixed with the soil, and afterwards in the form of generous annual mulches.

Opposite: *Clematis flammula* has myriads of almond-scented flowers (see page 68)

Left: *Actinidia deliciosa* is better known as the kiwi fruit (see page 60)

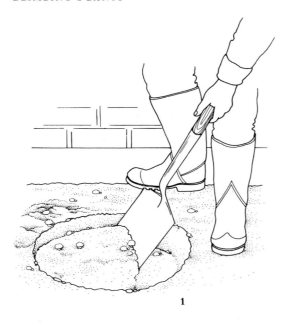

1

Planting a climber

1 Climbers growing on a wall need a good start in life, with a generous planting hole large enough to accommodate the rootball.

2 Break up the soil at the bottom of the hole and fork in plenty of compost or well-rotted manure.

2

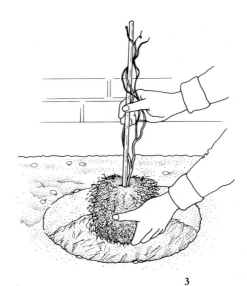

3

4

3 Position plant in hole so that soil level will correspond with soil level in container or soil mark on stem, in the case of a bare-rooted plant.

4 Backfill hole firming as you go and removing any large stones or rubble

Whatever the natural soil of your garden you will need to take especial care when planting climbers, particularly against house walls. The topsoil may have been removed or buried, and the remaining subsoil may be contaminated with rubble, cement and lime mortar. Furthermore, the soil at the foot of a wall is always drier than the soil in the open garden, and in the growing season especially wall-grown climbers may be severely stressed through lack of moisture. The more careful the initial preparation, the better the results. Climbers such as large flowered roses or clematis are expected to produce a great deal of flower, often over a long season, and need generous treatment at the root to give such abundant returns.

Climbers that you intend to decorate a host tree will also need more careful planting than those that are growing among shrubs, say; most trees have an extensive and thirsty root system with which your climber may have to compete. It is sometimes possible to plant the climber hard up against the host tree among the main anchoring roots – the feeding roots are found further out. The feeding root system extends, as a rule of thumb, as far underground as the spread of the tree's branches above; if a space cannot be found among the anchoring roots to prepare an adequate planting site, the alternative is to plant beyond the reach of the main network of roots and to lead the climber to the lowest branches by means by a stout string or a cane, at least until its own stems have made sufficient growth to hold it to its host.

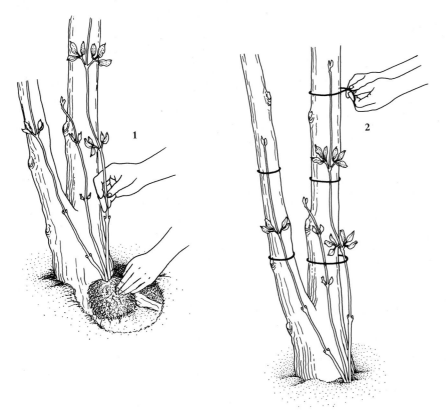

1 Climbers planted close up against a tree need a carefully prepared planting hole, enriched with compost or well-rotted manure, among the anchoring roots of the host.
2 Tie climber to host plant to guide it on its way

Though moisture is important, so too is drainage. Stagnant water at the roots spells death to most plants, and if your soil tends to become waterlogged you may need to lay drains, or to raise the soil above the general level. Sometimes, if the problem is not too severe, it can be solved by planting a shrub, such as a willow perhaps, which does not resent occasional waterlogging; in a fairly short time the willow will have developed an extensive root system which will absorb the excess moisture, and the climber can then be planted by its new host. I did this very successfully in one garden with *Salix elaeagnos*, which in two or three years grew large enough to act as host to a *Clematis viticella* hybrid, displaying its small violet flowers among the narrow grey leaves of the willow.

Once the site is suitably prepared, climbers can be planted like any other plant. Bare-rooted climbers can be planted in autumn or spring; hardy deciduous kinds can be planted in mild weather at any time from autumn to spring. The more tender the climber, the more important it is to plant it in spring rather than expect it to face its first winter when barely established after early autumn planting, and this is also true of evergreen climbers. The danger of spring drought, often a problem with planting at this season, is more easily overcome than the damage caused by a spell of severe weather to a newly planted, frost-tender plant. In any event, especially in the first season after planting, particular care should be taken not to allow climbers to become dry at the roots.

Container-grown climbers can be planted during the growing season and, provided that they are kept well watered and if necessary shaded from scorching sun, will often become established quickly and well in warm soil. Both bare-rooted and container-grown climbers should have their roots carefully teased out and the soil should be gently firmed; they should be thoroughly watered in after planting and again regularly afterwards while in growth.

Tender plants can be protected against frost and wind by bracken held between layers of chicken wire (left). Even conifer branches can give some protection (right). However, these may need to be pinned down with pegs or chicken wire if the situation is exposed

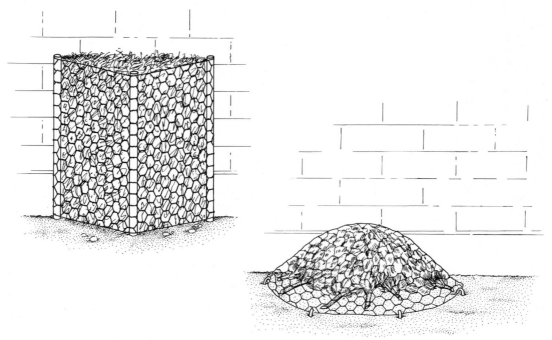

Protection against wind and frost may be needed, especially for the more tender climbers. Plants can be badly buffeted by wind even against walls – perhaps particularly against walls, where eddies may form. Wind also has a drying effect. Most damaging of all are freezing winds, which both chill and dessicate. Bracken, screens of chicken wire sandwiching bracken or straw, proprietary windscreening or even conifer branches can all be used, while the roots can be protected by a generous mulch of bark, peat, leaves, or grit.

Once established, climbers should receive an annual mulch of nutritious humus, or of peat or bark laced with fertilizer, to enable them to give of their best year after year.

Berberidopsis corallina (see page 62) needs a very sheltered site; in exposed areas this evergreen does really require the protection of glass

PRUNING AND TRAINING

Climbers are pruned for the same reasons, and according to the same commonsensical rules, as any other plant. One of the reasons is to keep the plant looking its best, encouraging it in its early stages of growth to form a sound, well-shaped framework that will fill its allotted space and, of course, to promote good crops of both flowers and fruit as appropriate. The pruning and training of climbers thus go hand in hand. Another reason is to keep the plant in good health by removing diseased or old and outworn growth. Then, as it advances in age, it may begin to outgrow its space, or to become over-luxuriant and need thinning.

Plants that flower on the current year's growths, generally those that flower after mid summer, should be pruned in late winter or early spring, so that the new growths have the longest possible growing period to form flowering shoots. Those that flower early in the year bear their flowers on growths from the previous year; these should be pruned immediately after they have flowered. Flowering shoots are removed and new growths will appear to carry next year's flowers.

Though I referred just now to 'rules', there are in fact no firm rules for pruning, other than the guidelines just suggested. One author will say that newly planted climbers should be only very lightly pruned until they have filled their intended space and formed their main framework of branches. Another

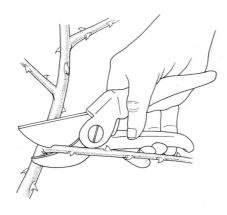

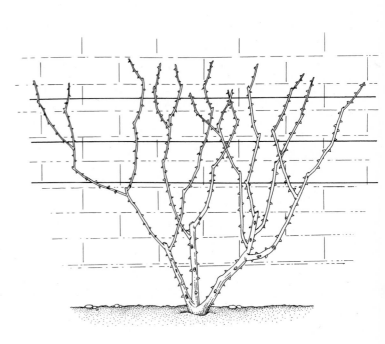

One important rule of pruning is to use good quality secateurs and keep them sharp and in good order. This will ensure all pruning cuts are clean with no snags or tears.

Climbing roses should be pruned to form a well-balanced framework of branches will belong to the school that recommends cutting the young climber back by half in the spring following planting, to encourage it to branch low down rather than become leggy. The rule about pruning immediately after flowering breaks down if we hope for attractive fruits to follow early flowers; if vigorously applied, this rule would deprive us of half the display.

The aim should always be to have the plant looking its best. If it is cluttered up with thin, spindly shoots, or marred by old and diseased growths, it will neither look good when not in flower nor produce the best crop of blooms that it could. A few plants will resent being cut hard back into old wood, but most respond well to sensible pruning. For example, an old, woody-stemmed clematis may die if cut down almost to ground level, or it may produce strong new growths. It would be better, almost always, to prune regularly and never to allow your climber to become bare legged, its superstructure depending on an ancient stem. However, if you doubt your ability to prune effectively, it is probably better to abstain. When in doubt, don't.

PROPAGATION

Propagation is another aspect of cultivation that some people shy away from. Though there are of course difficult plants needing specialized treatment, many climbers are easy to increase. It is very rewarding to raise new plants to swap with friends, to sell for local charities, or simply to have more of in the garden.

Propagation from seed
1 Sow seed in a proprietary seed compost, cover thinly with more compost and firm.
2 Seed pans are best watered from below to avoid washing the seeds to one side of the pot.
3 Stratification involves mixing seeds in moist sand and standing pot outside for the winter. Fine mesh chicken wire protects seeds from vermin

Propagation from seed

Nature's way of increasing plants is, generally, by seed. Many climbers can be raised from seed, not only annual kinds or those treated as annuals but also longer lived kinds, which take correspondingly longer to reach flowering size from seed.

Some climbers will come entirely, or reasonably, true from seed; others, cultivars and hybrids especially of course, will more likely not. To be sure of reproducing exactly the same cultivar or hybrid, you must propagate it vegetatively by one or other of the means described below.

It is almost always worth using a proprietary seed compost, if only because it will have been sterilized so that there will be fewer weed seedlings to contend with, and fewer problems with diseases or pests. The seeds can be sown in trays if you have enough of each kind of seed, or in crocked pots if you have only a few seeds of each climber. The compost should be lightly firmed, leaving a little gap between the surface and the rim of the pot. The seeds are sown thinly, and covered lightly, or not at all if they are very fine. After sowing, water in the seeds from below by standing the pot or tray in water, or from above with a fine rose. The first and last drops from the watering process always seem to do the most damage by disturbing the soil surface; this can be minimized by passing the can back and forth across the pot so that only at the middle of the swing does the water reach the pot itself. Very fine seeds are especially apt to get flooded into one side of the pot if watered from above, so watering in from beneath is preferable. After watering in, drain the pots or trays thoroughly and then stand them in a frame, a greenhouse or a shady windowsill to germinate.

Opposite: *Clematis rehderiana* (see page 69), like all species clematis, can be raised from seed as well as from internodal cuttings (see page 49)

Right: *Oxypetalum caeruleum* (see page 88), a twining perennial raised from seed

Some seeds, especially those with a fleshy covering such as a berry, may need a long period before germination, probably with alternating cold and warmth to break their dormancy. This applies particularly to woody plants, climbers included, from areas with severe winters. The dormancy of the seed is an adaptation designed to prevent the seeds germinating before the winter, which would be sure to kill the tender young seedlings. The simplest way to persuade such seeds to germinate is to sow them in autumn and leave them outside – protected against vermin – to endure any spells of frost that the winter may offer. Many will duly germinate the following spring. A slightly more sophisticated adaptation of this treatment is known as stratification. The seeds are mixed with moist sand and placed in layers between more sand in a pot or perforated container. The container is then set in a cold spot to get frosted and thawed during the winter. By late winter the seeds should be ready to sow in the usual way. The drawback to this method is that it is all too easy to forget to tip out the stratified seeds and sow them, so that often a few seeds will germinate in the sand, where they will quickly starve if not rescued; meanwhile, the others are probably wasted.

As soon as seedlings begin to appear they should be inspected regularly, daily if possible, given more light if they seem leggy, and pricked out individually the moment they are large enough to handle. After pricking out they are firmed, gently, and watered in. A proprietary potting compost will be suitable, or you can make your own. Whether the newly potted seedlings are stood in a frame or a cold greenhouse, or in heat, will depend on the species; naturally plants from warmer climates will need more cossetting than the frost-hardy kinds. As they grow, and the season advances, they are gradually hardened off before they are planted out, or potted on if they are slow-growing kinds needing more than one season to become large enough for their final positions.

Layering

Some climbers and sprawlers readily form roots from branches that touch the ground; the gardener's method of exploiting this to form new plants is known as layering. It is useful not only for increasing plants that easily form new roots in this way, but particularly also for rooting difficult plants that are hard to increase by cuttings. The chosen shoots can be rooted at ground level or by a method known as air layering. The first is the simpler. A suitable shoot, neither too soft and young nor old and woody, is selected and pegged down to the ground. To increase the chance of roots forming, a short, angled cut is made in the underside of the shoot, about a foot from the tip, and the cut area dusted with hormone rooting powder. The tip of the shoot is gently bent towards the vertical and tied to a bamboo, or it can be simply pegged down and left at an angle if there is any chance that bending it may sever the stem at the cut. It is usually worth mixing a little peat and sand with the natural soil at the point where the shoot is pegged down, to make a congenial mixture for the new roots to grow into. The shoot is left attached to the parent plant until well rooted, when it can be severed and either lifted and potted immediately, or left for a while to grow unsupported by the parent plant without also disturbing the roots, before being lifted and potted in the same way. Layering is not a quick method, but it may be the only way of putting roots on a particular plant.

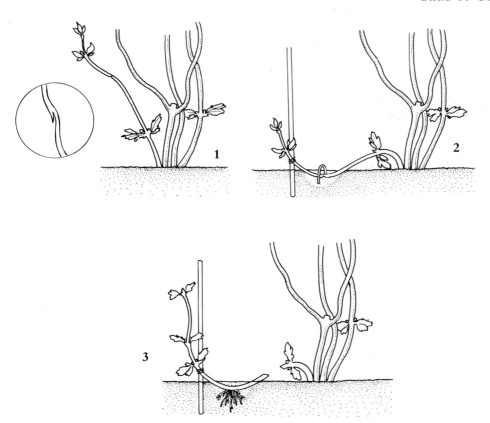

Layering and air-layering are variations on a theme; the method is often used for plants that do not root readily from cuttings

Layering
1 Choose a suitable stem and make an angled cut about 30 cm (12 in) from the tip. Dust wound with hormone rooting powder.
2 Bend stem so cut is pegged down in contact with the soil. Support tip of shoot with a stake.
3 When a root system is established the new plant can be severed from the parent

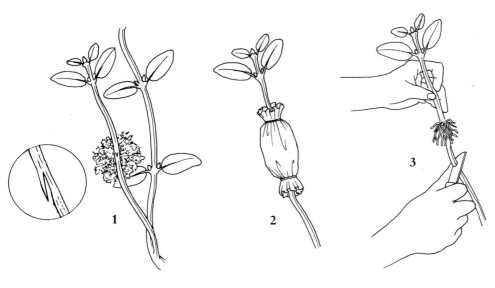

Air-layering
1 Cut stem and dust with hormone rooting powder. Wrap wound in damp sphagnum moss.
2 Tie a sleeve of polythene around the moss to keep it in place.
3 When roots have formed the new plant can be severed from its parent and potted up

Air layering

Air layering is resorted to when there are no suitable shoots near ground level that could be layered. The process is the same, except that the soil must be replaced by a suitable alternative, which is moist sphagnum moss tightly packed around the cut section of the stem. The moss is held in place with soft string or raffia and the whole thing wrapped in polythene to keep the moisture in. In time, all being well, roots will form and the shoot can be severed.

Some climbing plants can be divided or increased by digging up suckering stems. Brambles and smilax are but two examples of climbers which can be treated in this way

Division

Some climbers, especially herbaceous ones, can be increased by simple division. Some woody climbers spread by suckers, which can be removed to form new plants. These are usually removed with a sharp spade, leaving the stock plant undisturbed. True division, which applies to very few climbers, normally involves lifting the parent plant and teasing it apart – or forcing it apart with two forks back to back, if it is tough-rooted – just as with border plants. The divisions should be replanted immediately, or potted up to re-establish.

Cuttings

Lastly, we come to cuttings, probably the most artificial method of increasing plants and yet one of the most commonly used, especially where many plants are needed from one stock plant. Some plants root so easily that a shoot stuck in a glass of water will put out roots, while others are stubborn or even impossible to root without specialized equipment.

Cuttings may be made from stems or from roots, but unless specified as root cuttings (see page 49) the term usually means stem cuttings. These may be of two kinds, dormant or green and leafy.

Opposite:

Tropaeolum speciosum (see page 110) can be easily propagated from root cuttings (see pages 48 and 49)

Single bud cuttings

1 Cut stem into sections each bearing a single bud.
2 Press cuttings into cutting compost, lightly cover and place in a heated propagator

Root cuttings

1 Cut root into sections.
2 Prepared root cutting.
3 Insert thick root cuttings vertically.
4 Fine root cuttings can be 'sown' horizontally onto compost surface

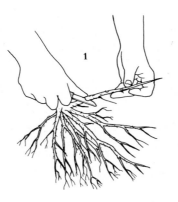

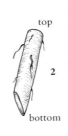

Soft or semi-ripe cuttings

1 Internodal cutting.
2 Heeled cutting.
3 Insert cuttings and water them in.
4 Cover with cling film to establish a humid environment for successful rooting

heel

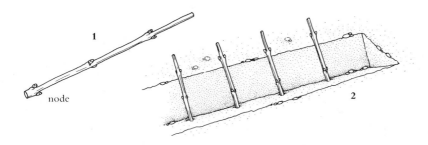

node

1

2

Hardwood cuttings
1 Prepared hardwood cutting
2 Cover cuttings with sandy soil so that only top third of stems are visible

Dormant or hardwood cuttings These are taken in autumn or early winter from mature shoots of the season, cut beneath a node and inserted to two-thirds their length in sandy soil in a sheltered, shaded spot. After a year the cuttings will normally be ready to lift and plant out.

Growing cuttings These will be soft or semi-hardwood. Soft cuttings, as the term implies, are taken from sappy young shoots early in the summer, or later provided that they are still soft. Semi-hardwood or semi-ripe cuttings are taken later in the season, when the shoots have begun to firm up. Both kinds may be taken with a heel of hardwood at the base or cut just below a node; in some cases, such as honeysuckles and, especially, clematis, they may be internodal cuttings, severed midway between two nodes. The lower leaves are removed with a sharp knife or razor and the remaining leaves may, if very large or very thin-textured, be reduced in size. The cuttings are inserted in a cutting compost, which may be half peat, half sharp sand, or may contain a proportion of Perlite or similar material. Some growers even like to root cuttings in pure Perlite or pure coarse sand, but they will need potting quickly once they have rooted or they will become starved and checked. Once inserted, the cuttings are carefully and thoroughly watered in, and then put in a frame, in a propagator, or under mist. Good results are often obtained by covering the cuttings with cling film, turned regularly to avoid too much build-up of condensation.

Hormone rooting powders may be used and are often especially useful for half-ripe cuttings. Softwood cuttings generally root quickly, if at all, without the need for hormone powders.

Single bud cutting A specialized type of stem cutting is the single bud cutting or eye, used for *Vitis* species. Well-formed buds with about 2 cm ($\frac{3}{4}$ in) of stem on either side are cut from mature stems in winter; a sliver of stem is removed from the side opposite the bud and the cut surface is pressed horizontally into a pot of cutting compost in a heated propagator.

Root cuttings These are sometimes used as a method of increase, especially for some herbaceous plants. Sections of root are inserted, the right way up, vertically or, if very fine, horizontally in pots or trays of cutting compost. After a while new shoots will grow, and later new roots from the base of the root cuttings. Comparatively few climbers are likely to be increased in this way, but it can be successfully used for campsis, for example.

4
Pests and Diseases

Compared to many plants, climbers are on the whole agreeably free from problems with pests and diseases. The best defence is good cultivation and good garden hygiene: plants that are growing strongly will resist diseases more easily than those that are stressed in any way, while if fallen leaves, dead branches and spent flowerheads are scrupulously removed many of the lurking places for pests, in particular, will be denied them.

PESTS

This is not to say, however, that climbers are entirely free of problems. Some may attack any climbers, while others are specific to certain genera. Common to many are **aphids**, of which **greenfly** and **blackfly** are the most abundant. Plants that are infested may be stunted and deformed, with fewer flowers than normal; honeysuckles are especially prone to suffer in this way. Aphids also exude sticky honeydew, which can ruin the foliage by encouraging sooty mould. Furthermore, aphids spread virus diseases (see page 53). It is well worth taking prompt action by spraying with a proprietary pesticide. If the aphids are concealed within curled leaves or among the perfoliate leaves and flower buds of honeysuckles, say, they will be hard to kill by contact sprays; a systemic insecticide will be more appropriate in these cases.

Aphids damage plants by sucking the sap from leaves and stems. Leaves may also be damaged by **capsid bugs**, which not only suck the sap from buds and young leaves but also kill the plant tissue where they feed, giving affected leaves their characteristic tattered appearance, with irregular small holes. Spraying with a suitable insecticide can control capsid bugs.

Pests that eat leaves include **caterpillars**, **earwigs** and **leafminers**; the last live inside the leaves and eat the tissues between the upper and lower surfaces, leaving a whitish trace as they tunnel through the leaf. Honeysuckles are often affected by leafminers; spraying with insecticide may be necessary. Earwigs can be trapped by the traditional method of filling a flowerpot with straw and upending it on top of a cane. Earwigs are most active on warm evenings, so each morning the flowerpot should be emptied and the earwigs destroyed.

Other pests are seen mainly on stems, though they also affect leaves: **scale insects** and the larvae of **froghoppers** among them. The latter can be seen as cuckoospit, frothy wet masses on young stems and leaves. Insecticide sprays can be used against these pests also.

A pest that is peculiar to roses is the **leaf-rolling rose sawfly**, which tightly rolls the leaflets of roses. Affected leaves can be picked off, or if necessary the pest can be controlled by a systemic insecticide.

Slugs can cause damage, especially to young growths; they are most active when the weather is damp. Slug pellets should be put down to protect susceptible growths. Damage at soil level may also be caused by cutworms, which can be controlled by dusting the soil with an insecticidal dust.

Opposite: A variegated cultivar of *Euonymus fortunei*, densely foliaged and evergreen

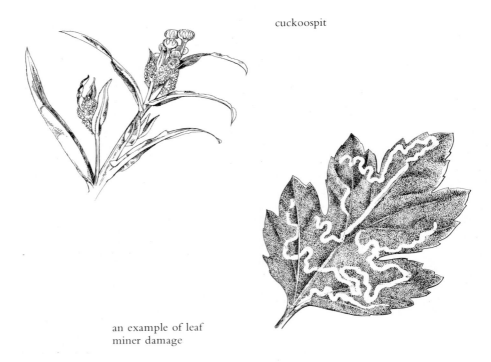

cuckoospit

an example of leaf
miner damage

Under glass **red spider mite** and **whitefly** are often troublesome. Red spider mites are sap suckers, often detected by the mottling and discoloration of affected leaves and sometimes by the fine silky web they weave. They thrive in warm, dry conditions, so high humidity can help to control them, or it may be necessary to spray with insecticide at frequent intervals. Whitefly, which resemble tiny white moths, can also be controlled by spraying. They cause similar damage to aphids, excreting honeydew which encourages sooty mould.

DISEASES

Many plant diseases are caused by a fungus of one kind or another. **Grey mould (*Botrytis*)** is a furry grey fungal growth especially difficult to control in wet seasons, while **powdery mildew**, a whitish powdery film on leaves, stems and buds, is worse when the soil is dry and is most troublesome in still conditions. Thus it is that rambler roses, many of which are particularly susceptible, should be grown not against a wall but in the open where the air can move freely through their stems. **Silverleaf**, a fungal disease most familiar in plums, may also affect honeysuckles. Grey mould and powdery mildew can be controlled by spraying with a suitable fungicide, while the affected parts of a plant attacked by silverleaf should be cut back to healthy tissue.

Two fungal diseases common to roses are **black spot** and **rust**. Spraying with suitable fungicides can help to control these diseases, though rust is still hard to control fully and badly affected plants should be dug up and burned. Both diseases can also be partially controlled by scrupulous hygiene; all fallen leaves, which harbour the disease, should be collected and burned.

Honey fungus can affect climbers, especially woody ones. The plant suddenly wilts and dies; when it is lifted, black bootlace-like rhizomorphs are often found on the roots of the affected plant. Various proprietary products are said to control honey fungus. Plants that are stressed, by drought or frost damage perhaps, seem much more susceptible than those that are growing strongly.

Clematis are apt to wilt and die suddenly from the notorious **clematis wilt**, which affects mainly large flowered cultivars. Sometimes only one or a few shoots are affected, sometimes the entire plant collapses. Any infected shoots should be cut right out and the remaining shoots, and the surrounding soil, sprayed regularly with benomyl. Beware slugs, too, which may attack the tender new shoots coming from below ground level as the plant makes new growth.

There are many **virus diseases** of plants, as of humans. Infected plants are stunted in growth and the leaves are often discoloured and misshapen. All such plants should be lifted and burnt. As already mentioned, controlling aphids helps to control virus diseases by limiting their spread.

black spot on rose

5
Climbing Plants for Greenhouse and Conservatory

It is, on the whole, for their spectacular flowers that we grow tender climbers needing the frost protection of a greenhouse or conservatory. Another attribute of many, though by no means all, is fragrance. Plants such as *Jasminum polyanthum* from China, or its counterparts from Australia, South Africa and Madeira, or night-scented *Hoya carnosa* (many plants are particularly fragrant at night) can fill a conservatory with perfume, the more powerful for being concentrated in the still air, not blown away by buffeting winds as so often happens outside. Others that are less intensely sweet may only reveal their scent when grown under glass – *Clematis cirrhosa* var. *balearica*, say.

Most of the fragrant climbers for greenhouses are white-flowered, but brightly coloured blooms are not lacking. The handsome family Bignoniaceae gives us flame-orange and scarlet, in *Doxantha*, *Pyrostegia* and *Tecomaria*.

Opposite: The magnificent conservatory at Flintham Hall in Nottinghamshire allows tender climbers to be displayed to best advantage

Left: *Bomarea kalbreyeri* has spectacular flowerheads (see page 64)

Bougainvilleas flaunt an amazing range of rich, vivid tones, from the typical strong magenta through scarlets and oranges and pinks to white. For yellows we can turn to *Hibbertia* and *Allamanda*, for blue-purples and violet-mauves to the passion flowers, while the morning glories offer many colours including pure azure blue. The pea family gives us the bright or sombre reds of *Kennedia* species and the rich violet of *Hardenbergia*. For deep, rich pink there are the dipladenias, and *Passiflora antioquiensis*.

Though such exotic blooms are welcome at any time of the year, perhaps the best time to enjoy flowers in the conservatory is in winter. At this time there will be flowers on *Canarina canariensis* and the African *Senecio tamoides*, discreet little *Clematis napaulensis* and perhaps, if the temperature is sufficiently high, *Jasminum polyanthum*. In late winter and spring appear the violet tassels of *Petraea volubilis* and the gorgeous flowers of *Pyrostegia venusta*, which surely gets its generic name from the flame-yellow colouring of its blooms.

In the lists of climbers that follow, more of those suitable for conservatories and greenhouses are native to South or Central America than to the other continents, though whether that merely reflects a personal bias I am not sure. From these regions come the passion flowers and the large, but little known, genus *Bomarea*, as well as much else. There are many jasmines, with representatives from Africa and Asia, the Azores and Australia; from Australia, too, we have some fine examples from the pea family. India, and the warmer regions of China and Burma, seem strangely ill represented, with only *Beaumontia*, from the first, and a jasmine, the giant honeysuckle and *Wattakaka sinensis* from southern China and Burma featuring in these pages.

CULTIVATION UNDER GLASS

Climbers are grown under glass according to the same principles as those out of doors, needing a well-nourished soil, ample moisture and due protection from pests and diseases. To these requirements we have to add temperature control and ventilation. Many climbers will grow well in containers, which will have the useful result of restricting their growth; but they will need much greater attention to watering and to feeding. Nutrients are rapidly leached out of the compost in a container that is adequately irrigated, and the available soil is in any case limited, so a regular feeding programme will be essential. To a lesser extent this is also true of climbers grown under glass in beds, whether at floor level or slightly raised.

In recognition of the high cost of keeping a greenhouse heated in winter, climbers such as stephanotis, which need high winter temperatures, are not mentioned in the lists that follow. Most of those that are will survive quite happily with winter minimum temperatures of 10–12°C (50–53°F); some will cope with a temperature range of 7–10°C (44–50°F), especially those that are dormant, and can be kept on the dry side, during the winter months.

Climbers under glass will need support, on wires or – for small-growing climbers – peasticks. Taller climbers that reach up to and across the roof have a utilitarian benefit quite apart from their beauty: they will shade the greenhouse in summer, so it may not be necessary to erect artificial shading or paint the glass. Very leafy climbers may even shade the greenhouse too much!

Climbers trained under glass can shade greenhouse plants from excessive sun in summer. The flowers and foliage can be trained to hang down in attractive festoons

Pruning

Pruning is the same as for climbers outside (see page 40), except that it may need to be carried out more often, and more severely, to keep the plants within bounds. A more scrupulous attention to hygiene will also be necessary; pests and diseases can build up with worrying rapidity under glass and those two chief pests of greenhouse plants, red spider mite and whitefly, can build up to plague levels if they are not controlled. Dead and fallen leaves and all dying or decaying material should regularly be removed from greenhouse plants, to minimize the risk of fungal diseases as well as for aesthetic reasons.

CLIMBERS WITH EDIBLE FRUIT

In the lists that follow there are some climbers that have edible fruit. Of those that need to be given frost protection, space could be given to *Passiflora edulis*, the passion fruit of greengrocers, or to the giant granadilla, *P. quadrangularis*. Hardier than these, but still worth greenhouse space, are the choicer varieties of grape vine. These are not named in the following pages, but can be obtained from specialist growers.

A to Z
of
Climbing
Plants

Climbing roses cascading over the wall at
The Botanical Garden, Oxford

ACONITUM Ranunculaceae

A. volubile From the Altai Mountains, this is a herbaceous twining climber bearing hooded blue-purple or lilac flowers in late summer and autumn on slender stems reaching to 3 m (10 ft) or more. A retentive soil is best, in sun or light shade. Propagate by division or from seed.

ACTINIDIA Actinidiaceae

A genus of mostly deciduous, twining climbers from eastern Asia. They can be successfully propagated by taking heel cuttings in late summer which root well with bottom heat.

A. arguta With great vigour, reaching 15 m (50 ft) or more, it has fragrant white flowers that appear in mid summer among shining, dark green foliage; the fruits that follow are edible but less tasty than those of *A. deliciosa*.

A. deliciosa This used to be called Chinese gooseberry until clever marketing transformed it into the kiwi fruit. Growing vigorously to 9 m (30 ft) or so, it has fragrant white flowers ageing to creamy buff and followed by the familiar brown, furry, green-fleshed fruits. Named cultivars bear larger fruits than the species; male and female plants are needed for a crop of fruit. Also known as *A. chinensis*.

A. kolomikta Grown for the colouring of its heart-shaped leaves, which are often – but not invariably – half green, half cream flushed with pink. The best colour comes from plants on sunny walls. Protect it against cats, which chew it as they will catmint and *Valeriana phu*.

A. polygama Less vigorous than *A. kolomikta*, its white or creamy variegation earns it the name silver vine.

ADLUMIA Papaveraceae

A. fungosa A pretty biennial climber with finely dissected leaves and pinky-mauve flowers shaped like those of a corydalis. It needs shade, and shelter from wind, to protect the delicate foliage from scorching. Sow *in situ* or individually in pots.

AKEBIA Lardizabalaceae

Two species of twining climbers from Japan and China. Propagate by layering or from cuttings.

A. quinata Semi-evergreen with attractive leaves each with five leaflets, and drooping racemes of chocolate-maroon, spicily scented flowers in spring. They combine delightfully with the dusty pink flowers of *Clematis macropetala* 'Markham's Pink'.

A. trifoliata Deciduous, and much less common than *A. quinata*, it has three leaflets in place of five, and similar flowers. Hybrids between the two have been named *A. × pentaphylla*. Any reasonable soil suits akebias, and they will twine over fences, pergolas, walls or shrubs with equal ease.

ALLAMANDA Apocynaceae

A. cathartica From Central and South America, it belongs to a family that gives us several beautiful tender greenhouse climbers. This one has rich yellow, trumpet-shaped flowers in clusters during summer and autumn, and can be grown in a tub to restrict its growth. Tie in the main stems and allow flowering growths to arch free. Cuttings root well with bottom heat.

AMPELOPSIS Vitaceae

Deciduous climbers from North America and Asia grown chiefly for their foliage. They climb by twining stem tendrils. Take cuttings in late summer.

A. aconitifolia Especially elegant, finely cut, shining green foliage.

A. brevipedunculata (*Vitis heterophylla*) From north-eastern Asia, it is striking when, after a long hot summer, it is decked with porcelain-blue fruits.

A. brevipedunculata 'Elegans' Much less vigorous, its leaves heavily splashed with cream and pink. It may be grown as a weakly garden plant, or in a pot.

A. megalophylla This has the largest leaves of any vine in cultivation, as much as 45–60 cm (18–24 in) long, deep green above and bluish-green beneath. It is vigorous in rich soils, to 8 or 9 m (26–30 ft).

ANREDERA Basellaceae

A. cordifolia From South America, formerly known as *Boussingaultia basilloides*. It is a tender, tuberous-rooted, twining climber with little white, mignonette-scented flowers opening in autumn. Readily propagated from the small aerial tubers that form in the non-flowering leaf axils.

APIOS Leguminosae

A. tuberosa A tuberous-rooted herbaceous climber, grown occasionally for its fragrant, blood red and lilac-brown pea-flowers, borne in autumn. The tubers are edible; the plant was introduced to Europe from eastern North America at about the same time as the true potato from South America. Propagate by division of the tubers.

ARAUJIA Asclepiadaceae

A. sericofera From South America, known as the cruel plant from the way in which night-flying moths are sometimes trapped by their tongues in the white or pink-mauve flowers, which appear in late summer. This twining evergreen is easily and quickly raised from seed and is hardier than sometimes supposed.

ARISTOLOCHIA Aristolochiaceae

This large and mainly tropical genus contains a few unusual and interesting hardy or near-hardy twining climbers, with curiously bent, tubular flowers. Propagate from seed or raise from cuttings taken in summer. To succeed the cuttings need the benefit of bottom heat and benefit from being grown in a propagating case.

A. californica This has purplish flowers, and the closely related *A. tomentosa* has yellow-green flowers with brown throats.

A. chrysops Rare, and the most striking of the genus. It has yellow flowers with maroon or black-purple lobes.

A. elegans From Brazil, a tender species. It bears a long succession of wide-mouthed, maroon, white-blotched flowers.

A. macrophylla The original dutchman's pipe, with yellow-green flowers, the lobes edged with madder brown, among handsome pale green, kidney-shaped leaves. Also known as *A. sipho*, it originates from eastern North America, and is the hardiest of these five species.

Aconitum volubile
(see page 60)

ASTERANTHERA Gesneriaceae

A. ovata One of the choice band of occasionally hardy woody gesneriads. An evergreen root-climber, it thrives in warm, damp shade in acid soil, conditions similar to those it enjoys in its native Chile, where it grows up tree trunks in dense forest. The tubular flowers, with five flared lobes, are rich pinkish-red and appear from mid summer onwards. Raise from cuttings.

BEAUMONTIA Apocynaceae

B. grandiflora From India, another exotic, tender member of the periwinkle family, a twining climber with long, fragrant, white trumpets borne in terminal trusses. It needs cool greenhouse treatment and can be grown in a pot in a peaty compost.

BERBERIDOPSIS Flacourtiaceae

B. corallina The coral plant, an evergreen climber from Chile. Among rich green, rather holly-like foliage, the hanging crimson flowers open from buds like beads of blood during summer and autumn. A neutral or acid soil, and shade in a sheltered site are needed. Propagates easily from cuttings.

BERCHEMIA Rhamnaceae

A genus of deciduous twining climbers with insignificant greenish flowers, unexciting unless the fruits form, which is rare in cooler climates. Take cuttings in late summer.

B. racemosa Hardy and vigorous with somewhat heart-shaped leaves, glaucous beneath. The fruits, when they

appear, are red ripening to black. A cream-splashed variegated form, 'Variegata', is known. Ordinary soil in sun or light shade is suitable.

BIGNONIA Bignoniaceae

Most of the climbers that used to be called *Bignonia* have been moved into other genera, notably *Campsis*, and only one species now remains. Raise from seed or soft cuttings.

B. capreolata The cross vine, from south-eastern United States. It is an evergreen or semi-evergreen tendril climber which needs support. It will scramble to 7 m (23 ft) and bears orange-red flowers of the typical flared trumpet shape of the family, but needs plenty of sun to flower freely.

BILLARDIERA Pittosporaceae

Tender Australian and Tasmanian climbers with slender, twining stems and delightful little bell-shaped flowers of lime green.

B. longifolia The most familiar species, whose flowers are followed by oblong berries, commonly dark blue but also sometimes red, purple or

white. They look like fleshy berries but are dry inside, the seeds rattling when the fruits are shaken. New plants can be easily raised from these seeds.

BOMAREA Alstroemeriaceae

A large genus of climbing alstroemerias with twining or scrambling stems, tuberous roots and tubular flowers. They need sun and ordinary soil, and a warm position, or grow well in containers in a cool greenhouse. All the bomareas are from South America, and can be divided to make new plants or raised from seed.

B. caldasii Yellow flowers flushed orange, or wholly orange or red, with greenish-brown spotting on the inner petals.

Allamanda cathartica growing in the wild (see page 60)

Campsis × tagliabuana 'Madame Galen' (see page 65)

B. × cantabrigiensis An uncommon hybrid of rather more subfusc colouring.

B. kalbreyeri A name that has been attached to *B. caldasii*, but it is a closely related species. The plant I grew under this name had spectacular orange flowers in huge heads.

Bougainvillea glabra

BOUGAINVILLEA Nyctaginaceae

Anyone familiar with the south of France, California, or indeed any other warm country where plants are appreciated, must know *Bougainvillea*. The colourful bracts that make the display are usually vivid magenta, but also come in coppery-orange or lighter shades of tangerine, pink, white, scarlet and crimson. Bougainvilleas thrive in greenhouse conditions and need comparatively little heat in winter. Raise from cuttings in summer.

CALYSTEGIA Convolvulaceae

Despite its beauty in flower, no one would voluntarily grow the common white bindweed; most of us spend hours trying to eradicate it and its lesser cousins. Propagate by division.

C. pubescens From Japan, a beautiful herbaceous climber with double pink flowers. It needs a rich soil and a warm climate to thrive.

CAMPSIS Bignoniaceae

Showy, deciduous, self-clinging climbers with pinnate foliage, the trumpet vines need hot summers to flower effectively; plant them on a sunny wall. Take cuttings in late summer.

C. grandiflora From China, this has the largest flowers and needs a little help to cling to its support. The flowers are orange in the throat, with flared, apricot-orange lobes.

C. radicans A firm self-clinger with scarlet-lobed flowers. From southeastern United States , it needs a good deal of sun. It has a beautiful yellow form, 'Flava', which deserves a hot and sunny wall to encourage its exquisite soft yellow flowers.

C. × tagliabuana 'Madame Galen'
A hybrid between the Chinese and the
American species, this is most suitable
for a temperate climate, and spectacular in flower when well set with its
salmon-orange trumpets.

CANARINA Campanulaceae

C. canariensis A tender, tuberous-
rooted bellflower endemic to the
Canary Islands. Easily raised from seed
in a cool greenhouse, it bears its waxy
orange bells from late autumn to
spring and dies down in mid summer,
when it can be dried off. Start into
growth again after repotting in late
summer and keep moist during its
growing season.

CARDIOSPERMUM Sapindaceae

C. halicacabum A tender perennial
from the pantropics, grown as an
annual. The first two flower buds are
modified into tendrils, the remainder
opening to tiny white flowers followed by balloon-like capsules con-
taining the seeds. These are black,
with a white, heart-shaped mark,
giving the plant its botanical name.

CELASTRUS Celastraceae

Belonging to the same family as the
spindle trees, these vigorous twining
climbers bear bright seeds of scarlet
and yellow. The hardy species are
deciduous; the two best known, described here, bear male and female
flowers on separate plants so one of
each sex is needed for the showy fruits
to be formed.

C. orbiculatus From north-eastern
Asia, this has a hermaphrodite form,
which should produce a good crop of
scarlet-seeded, glossy yellow fruits.

C. scandens From North America,
not so free-fruiting; no hermaphrodite form is known. The fruits,
when they do appear, are orange with
scarlet seeds.

CISSUS Vitaceae

These are mainly tropical vines, some
of which are familiar as house plants.
Propagate from seed or take cuttings
in summer.

C. antarctica The kangaroo vine,
which has copious, glossy green,
toothed foliage.

C. rhombifolia From Mexico to
Brazil, this is another popular house
plant, with shining, dark green,
trifoliate leaves.

C. striata Nearly hardy outside in
mild areas. A vigorous, evergreen,
tendril climber from Brazil and Chile,
it has leathery, shiny green, deeply
divided leaves on elegant, zig-zag
stems.

CLEMATIS Ranunculaceae

A large genus of climbers (and a few
non-climbing types, not mentioned
here) of which many are deciduous
and some – the less hardy – are
evergreen. Clematis can be found in
flower for nine or ten months of the
year. Take internodal cuttings; species
can be propagated from seed.

The pruning of clematis is a subject
that exercises many gardeners, though
– as with pruning in general –
common sense and a knowledge of the
flowering season of the plant will
resolve many doubts. Several books
on clematis have been written and full
notes on pruning can be found in
these. Here, I will follow Christopher
Lloyd in applying a simple rule of
thumb, thus:

□ **Group I** Clematis that flower in spring need to be pruned only if space is limited; if so, all the flowering shoots should be cut out just after flowering.

□ **Group II** These are the early-flowering, large flowered hybrids that produce their first flowers before mid June. Cut out all dead growths, and in February–March shorten all the remaining stems to the first pair of strong buds, which will then be fat and green.

□ **Group III** Late-flowering clematis, starting into flower after mid June and perhaps right into the autumn. Cut all the growths hard back, to 1 m (3 ft) or less, in February–March.

I have divided the clematis lists into two parts: first, species, with a few hybrids that resemble species; second, a selection from among the hundreds of large flowered hybrids that are described in nurserymen's catalogues.

SPECIES

C. aethusifolia From China, with beautiful ferny, pale green foliage on modest growth, and nodding, pale yellow bells in late summer, followed by feathery white seedheads. □ Group III.

C. alpina From northern Europe and northern Asia, flowering in spring; the flowers are lantern-shaped, in shades of blue, white or reddish, and are followed by grey-white seedheads.

'Columbine' is pale blue, 'Pamela Jackman' deep blue and 'Frances Rivis' the largest-flowered blue. 'Ruby' is deep pink. A newer cultivar is 'Willy', pale pink inside and darker outside. 'White Columbine' is of course white, as is 'White Moth'; other whites are now thought to be forms of *C. macropetala*. Newer, rich purple-blues are 'Helsingbord' and 'Tage Lundell'. □ All Group I.

Opposite: *Clematis tangutica* (see page 69)

Right: *Celastrus orbiculatus* (see page 65)

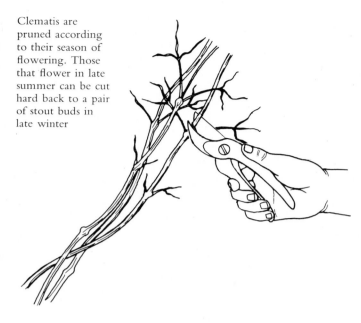

Clematis are pruned according to their season of flowering. Those that flower in late summer can be cut hard back to a pair of stout buds in late winter

C. armandii From China, with bold evergreen foliage and sprays of white, vanilla-scented flowers in spring. Named forms are the larger-flowered 'Snowdrift', and pink-budded 'Apple Blossom'. □ Group I.

C. australis From New Zealand, this is a somewhat tender evergreen species, with finely cut foliage and fragrant, creamy-green, starry flowers in spring. □ Group I.

C. campaniflora From Portugal and southern Spain. The small, wide-open bells of white, suffused milky mauve, appear in late summer. □ Group III.

C. chrysocoma This Chinese species is shrubby, but a plant in cultivation under this name is a vigorous climber of the C. montana type, with well-shaped, soft pink flowers and downy foliage (described by the specific name which means 'golden haired'). C. chrysocoma var. sericea (C. spooneri) has white flowers and less downy foliage. Spring-flowering. □ Group I.

C. cirrhosa From southern Europe; like its Balearic Islands form C. cirrhosa var. balearica, flowers in mild weather throughout the winter. The nodding, bell-shaped flowers are greenish-cream, freckled inside with warm brown. Variety balearica has very finely cut foliage, giving it its name of fern-leaved clematis; the leaves turn bronze in winter. It is also known as C. calycina. □ Group I.

C. connata From the Himalayas and south-western China, this resembles the better-known C. rehderiana, with narrow, Naples yellow (soft buff yellow) bells in autumn. □ Group III.

C. crispa An uncommon species from south-eastern United States, resembling in flower the herbaceous, 'hyacinth-flowered' C. heracleifolia. The pale blue-mauve flowers appear in summer. □ Group II.

C. fargesii var. **souliei** A vigorous species allied to the British native C. vitalba, old man's beard. It bears its white flowers, which are much larger than those of C. vitalba, freely in summer. □ Group III.

C. flammula A European species with myriads of small, white, almond-scented flowers in large clusters in late summer and autumn. □ Group III.

C. florida 'Plena' The exquisite double, greenish-white form of a Chinese species that has been the parent of many large flowered hybrids. □ Group II.

C. florida 'Sieboldii' (C. florida var. bicolor) is not a robust grower, but worth perseverance for its passion-flower-like blooms, white with a great central boss of violet-purple stamens. □ Group II.

C. fosteri From New Zealand, this has

creamy-green flowers in spring, with a scent of lemon verbena, among bright apple green foliage. ☐ Group I.

C. indivisa see *C. paniculata*.

C. × jouiniana A vigorous hybrid between *C. heracleifolia* var. *davidiana*, an herbaceous species, and *C. vitalba*. A non-clinging scrambler, it has massed, pale lavender, hyacinth-like flowers in late summer. 'Praecox' begins to flower earlier and has a longer season.

C. macropetala From China, allied to *C. alpina* and as hardy, with fuller, semi-double flowers in spring. The type is blue-violet, and a good named selection is 'Maidwell Hall'; 'Lagoon' is another to look out for. 'Snowbird' is white; 'Harry Smith' is pale blue. The dusty pink 'Markham's Pink' and the newer, full-flowered pink 'Ballet Skirt' complete the set. ☐ Group I.

C. montana From the Himalayas and western China, a very vigorous spring-flowering species. The type is white; var. *rubens* has purple-tinted young foliage and pink-mauve flowers. Similar to this is 'Picton's Variety'. 'Tetrarose' is a tetraploid form, with larger, deeper rosy-mauve flowers and bronzed foliage. Much paler is 'Vera', in soft pink with a sweet scent, as has 'Elizabeth', which fades to near-white in shade. 'Grandiflora' is a larger-flowered white. ☐ All Group I.

C. napaulensis A charming, rather tender, winter-flowering species from Nepal, allied to *C. cirrhosa* and bearing creamy-yellow, purple-stamened bells. ☐ Group I.

C. orientalis A name encountered more often than the true plant itself. 'Orange Peel', and the Ludlow and Sherriff plant L. & S. 13342, are both referable to the Himalayan *C. tibetana*

subsp. *vernayi*. All the plants in this group have lantern-shaped flowers often with thick-textured petals, yellow or greenish-yellow and borne in summer and autumn, the later flowers among the silky, wig-like seed heads of the earlier blooms. ☐ Group III.

C. paniculata The correct name for the clematis still often labelled *C. indivisa*, a beautiful New Zealand evergreen for a warm wall with bright white flowers in late spring. ☐ Group I.

C. phlebantha From Nepal, with silky, silvery foliage on trailing stems, and white, red-veined flowers in summer. Still uncommon and perhaps not entirely hardy, but well worth seeking out. ☐ Group I.

C. rehderiana From western China, it has nodding, primrose-yellow, cowslip-scented, tubular bells among downy foliage, on vigorous growth. Late summer- and autumn-flowering. ☐ Group III.

C. serratifolia Allied to *C. orientalis*. From China and Korea, it has straw-yellow flowers with madder-brown stamens and a pleasing lemon fragrance. Summer into autumn. ☐ Group III.

C. tangutica This is a brighter yellow, lantern-flowered species, from north-west India and China. Vigorous and easy in sun or shade, and as decorative in white, silky seed as in flower. ☐ Group III. A hybrid between this and *C. tangutica* subsp. *obtusiuscula* is 'Bill MacKenzie' with larger, bright yellow flowers. 'Corry' is a cross between subsp. *obtusiuscula* and *C. tibetana* subsp. *vernayi*, and has thick-petalled, flared bells of clear yellow. ☐ Group III.

Clematis vitalba

C. texensis From the southern United States, more or less herbaceous, with red or purple nodding bells in summer. It is the parent of several beautiful hybrids, all worth seeking out.

'Duchess of Albany' Upright, tulip-shaped flowers of deep pink.
☐ Group III.

'Etoile Rose' Also herbaceous. The flowers are cherry-purple, nodding bells, each tepal edged silvery-pink.
☐ Group III.

'Gravetye Beauty' Cherry-crimson flowers, narrow bells flaring to a starry shape, in summer. ☐ Group III.

'Pagoda' Pale pink-lilac, nodding flowers with outward-curving petal tips. ☐ Group III.

'Sir Trevor Lawrence' Rare and desirable, with cherry-red, cream-stamened flowers. ☐ Group III.

Clematis texensis
'Pagoda'

C. tibetana subsp. vernayi Beautiful glaucous-blue foliage sets off nodding, yellow-green flowers in late summer.
☐ Group III.

C. × vedrariensis (*C. chrysocoma* × *C. montana* var. *rubens*) A vigorous climber with the hairy foliage of the

first and the rose-pink flowers and bronzed leaves of the second parent.
☐ Group I.

C. vitalba The native old man's beard or traveller's joy, an extremely vigorous plant with small flowers scarcely suitable for the garden.

C. viticella A slender European species with nodding, violet-blue flowers on long stalks. It is the parent of many hybrids, of which the following retain some of the charm of the species.

'Abundance' Semi-nodding wine-rose flowers in summer. ☐ Group III.

'Alba Luxurians' White flowers, green-tipped and dark-centred, summer onwards. ☐ Group III.

'Etoile Violette' Deep violet, summer onwards. ☐ Group III.

'Little Nell' Creamy-white flowers, each tepal edged in mauve. Summer.
☐ Group III.

'Minuet' White flowers edged and veined in mauve, semi-nodding.
☐ Group III.

'Purpurea Plena Elegans' Double rosette-shaped flowers of soft, dusty grey-purple. An old, recently resuscitated double to look out for is 'Mary Rose', with violet-blue rosettes backed with silvery blue. Group III.

'Royal Velours' Rich velvety purple flowers. ☐ Group III.

'Rubra' ('Kermesiana') Claret-red – rather a blue claret. ☐ Group III.

'Venosa Violacea' Purple tepals fading to white at the centre, veined purple. Summer. ☐ Group III.

LARGE FLOWERED HYBRIDS

'Barbara Dibley' Petunia red, bleaching in bright sun; early-flowering. ☐ Group II.

'Beauty of Worcester' Double deep blue with cream anthers, early; later flowers are single. ☐ Group II.

'Comtesse de Bouchaud' Showy, bright mauve-pink flowers abundantly borne late in the season. ☐ Group III.

'Daniel Deronda' Early flowers are especially large; semi-double, deep violet with creamy anthers. Later flowers are single. ☐ Group II.

'Duchess of Edinburgh' Double white flowers sometimes suffused with green. ☐ Group II.

'Elsa Späth' Large, rich blue flowers over a long season. ☐ Group II.

'Ernest Markham' Perhaps the best red clematis, with rich magenta blooms; full sun. ☐ Group II.

'Gipsy Queen' Large, velvet purple flowers with red anthers; late. ☐ Group III.

Clematis montana 'Elizabeth' (see page 69)

'**Hagley Hybrid**' Well-shaped, warm mauve flowers with madder red anthers; late. ☐ Group III.

'**Henryi**' Old but still beautiful, creamy-white enhanced by chocolate anthers. ☐ Group II.

'**Huldine**' Mother-of-pearl white, flushed mauve on the reverse. ☐ Group III.

'**Jackmanii Superba**' By far the best-known large flowered clematis, with dark, velvety, violet blooms. Vigorous and easy. ☐ Group III.

'**Lady Betty Balfour**' Rich purple fading towards blue; late. ☐ Group III.

'**Lady Northcliffe**' Clear, porcelain blue with white anthers, free flowering. ☐ Group II.

'**Lasurstern**' Striking blue-violet flowers with creamy anthers. ☐ Group II.

'**Marie Boisselot**' ('Madame le Coultre') Wonderful large white flowers with pale anthers. ☐ Group II.

'**Mrs Cholmondeley**' Large, light blue-mauve flowers with gaps between the tepals, produced over a long season in great abundance. ☐ Group II.

'**Nelly Moser**' Almost as well known as 'Jackmanii Superba', and one of several with pale mauve flowers, each sepal with a deeper magenta-lilac bar. ☐ Group II.

'**Niobe**' Deepest velvety crimson. ☐ Group III.

'**Perle d'Azur**' Periwinkle-blue flowers with cream anthers; specially lovely and unaccountably hard to acquire. ☐ Group III.

'**Star of India**' Free-flowering, with plum purple tepals each with a deep carmine red bar. ☐ Group III.

'**The President**' A long season of violet-purple flowers with silvery reverse. ☐ Group II.

'**Ville de Lyon**' Bright carmine, late-flowering. ☐ Group III.

'**Vyvyan Pennell**' Fine double lavender-blue flowers; later flowers are single. ☐ Group II.

'**W. E. Gladstone**' Very large, lavender blue flowers. Group II.

'**William Kennet**' An old kind with lavender blue flowers, red anthers. ☐ Group II.

'**Yellow Queen**' ('Moonlight') Exquisite creamy flowers, sometimes appearing to be almost primrose. ☐ Group II.

CLEMATOCLETHRA Actinidiaceae

No relation of *Clematis* (nor indeed of *Clethra*) as the family name indicates, this is a genus of deciduous climbers of Asian origin.

C. integrifolia Fragrant white flowers appear in summer among green, bristle-edged foliage that is glaucous beneath.

C. lasioclada Similar to *C. integrifolia*, with clusters of white flowers in summer.

C. scandens Brown, bristly young shoots and leaves glaucous beneath; small white flowers in summer are followed by red berries.

CLITORIA Leguminosae

C. mariana This fine climber from southern United States and Mexico can be grown in a greenhouse or raised from seed each year as an annual. It is of modest stature and bears its lilac flowers during the summer.

COBAEA Cobaeaceae

C. scandens Another Mexican climber which can be treated as a perennial in a greenhouse or grown as an annual to produce in one season its fat-belled flowers. These are greenish-white, deepening to violet; 'Alba' remains white throughout.

CODONOPSIS Campanulaceae

A delightful genus of (mainly) twining herbaceous climbers, many tuberous-rooted and some smelling of fox (or garlic) – much the same smell as the crown imperial (*Fritillaria imperialis*). All are from Asia. A cool soil in partial shade, with some shelter, suits *Codonopsis*.

C. clematidea Nodding bells of milky blue, exquisitely marked within with maroon rings, in summer.

C. convolvulacea Close to or even synonymous with *C. vinciflora*; the first name conveys the twining nature, the second the wider-open flowers, of periwinkle blue. Variety *forrestii* is larger in flower.

C. tangshen Green bells with a purple flush, and purple inner markings.

C. viridiflora A yellower green, with purple spots at the base.

CONVOLVULUS Convolvulaceae

C. althaeoides A trailing and twining herbaceous perennial with greyish foliage and rosy-pink, satiny, saucer-shaped flowers in summer. Mediterranean region. Propagate from soft cuttings.

C. elegantissimus From the eastern Mediterranean, this is similar, with silky, silvery foliage. Both can become a little invasive, needing a low but wide-spreading shrub to ramble through.

CUCURBITA Cucurbitaceae

Cucurbita pepo From Mexico and south-western United States, this is the vegetable marrow; *C. pepo* var. *ovifera* is the ornamental gourd, producing its fruits of varied shape – round, flagon-shaped and so on – often brightly coloured and striped in yellows and greens, smooth or warty. They are hard-skinned and can be dried for decoration. Raise annually from seed.

DECUMARIA Hydrangeaceae

Woody, root-clinging climbers related to the hydrangea. Raise from late-summer cuttings.

D. barbara From south-eastern United States, deciduous, with glossy foliage and clusters of white, fragrant flowers in summer. For a sheltered site only.

D. sinensis A Chinese species, it is one of the few hardy self-clinging evergreens, with attractive shiny foliage and cream, honey-scented flowers in summer.

DICENTRA Fumariaceae

The bleeding heart or lady in the bath, *D. spectabilis*, has some charming climbing relatives with similar heart- or locket-shaped flowers. All are herbaceous, and climb by tendrils at the leaf-tips. Raise from seed.

D. chrysantha A Californian species with pale, glaucous, much-divided foliage and bright yellow flowers held – exceptionally for the genus – in erect clusters in summer. For light soils in sun.

DICHELOSTEMMA Alliaceae

D. volubilis Another Californian plant, and an oddity in its climbing habit; for it has a corm, and is related to the familiar *Brodiaea*. Drooping pink flowers are borne in summer on long twining stems. A light soil, sun, and frost protection are needed.

DIPLADENIA see **Mandevilla**

DOLICHOS see **Lablab**

DOXANTHA Bignoniaceae

D. unguis-cati The cat's-claw vine climbs by means of tendrils equipped with tiny, tenacious hooks. The bright yellow flowers are of typical bignonia shape and appear in late spring and summer. Take cuttings in summer.

ECCREMOCARPUS Bignoniaceae

E. scaber From Chile, though in the *Bignonia* family, this does not have the characteristic flared trumpets; instead the flowers are lopsidedly bottle-shaped. Typically orange, they are rich scarlet-crimson in var. *carmineus* and amber-yellow in var. *aureus*. The divided foliage is green, or bronzed in the red-flowered form. Slightly tender, the plant is often cut to the ground in winter but usually reappears; it is so easily raised from seed to flower in the first year that its loss is no tragedy. It climbs by leaf tendrils.

Opposite:
Eccremocarpus scaber

Left: *Decumaria sinensis* (see page 73)

ERCILLA Phytolaccaceae

E. volubilis (*Bridgesia spicata*) An uncommon Chilean, self-clinging, evergreen climber with pleasant deep green foliage and dense spikes of small, whitish-purple flowers in spring. Slightly tender. Propagate by layering or from late-summer cuttings.

EUONYMUS Celastraceae

E. fortunei var. radicans A root-clinging climber with evergreen foliage, much cultivated in its fancy variegated forms, which may never adopt their adult, non-climbing state (cf. *Hedera*, ivy). Forms with yellow or cream variegations are available under a variety of by no means consistent names. 'Coloratus' refers to a vigorous kind that turns an attractive maroon-

purple in winter. Take cuttings in summer or autumn.

FICUS Moraceae

One climbing member of this large family is cultivated in cool temperate areas.

F. pumila A native of the Far East, this evergreen needs sheltered conditions; it will stand dense shade. The root-clinging stems are set with small, heart-shaped leaves. This plant has juvenile and shrubby adult stages. Take cuttings in summer.

GELSEMIUM Loganiaceae

G. sempervirens This jasmine-like climber is actually of the same family as *Buddleia*. From south-eastern United States and Central America, it is scarcely frost-resistant, needing cool greenhouse conditions. A twining evergreen, with lustrous, narrow leaves, it bears clusters of trumpet-shaped, sweetly scented, pale to deep yellow flowers in summer. Raise from seed or take cuttings in summer.

GLORIOSA Liliaceae

G. superba The glory lily has tuberous roots and slender stems with narrow, shining leaves tipped with little hooks. The nodding flowers, like exotic turkscap lilies, are yellow ageing to red. It is often listed as *G. rothschildiana*, a form that has crimson flowers edged with yellow. Eastern Asia and tropical Africa. Store the tubers in warmth during winter. Propagate by seed, by division of the tubers or by offsets.

HARDENBERGIA Leguminosae

The pea family is rich in rather tender,

Gelsemium sempervirens

beautiful climbers. Take cuttings in summer or sow seed.

H. violacea From eastern Australia and Tasmania, with evergreen foliage and sprays of violet pea-flowers in spring. Pink and white forms exist. Requires a cool greenhouse where there is any likelihood of frost.

HEDERA Araliaceae

A genus of self-clinging evergreen climbers with a mature state of shrubby nature on which flowers and fruits are borne. There are few species and dozens of cultivars, selected for their variegated or strikingly shaped leaves. Raise from cuttings.

H. canariensis From the Canary Islands, the Azores and north-west Africa, it has large, heart-shaped leaves on red stems. 'Gloire de Marengo' is a popular, slightly tender cultivar with green and silvery-grey leaves edged with cream.

H. colchica The Persian ivy is native to the Caucasus, Turkey and northern Iran. The large, leathery leaves are borne on green stems, or brown-purple in 'Dentata'. 'Dentata Variegata' has bold, creamy-yellow, variegated foliage; 'Sulphur Heart' or 'Paddy's Pride' has the reverse variegation, the centre primrose yellow instead of the margins.

H. helix The British, European and western Asian ivy which has given rise to so many cultivars, many grown as house plants though most will survive a few degrees of frost.
'Buttercup' All yellow, turning to lime or even green in shade but burning easily in sun, so none too easy to please.
'Glacier' An old variegated cultivar, silvery-grey and cream.

'Glymii' Green in summer, blackish-purple in winter.
'Goldheart' ('Jubilee') This cultivar has bright splash of yellow in the centre of each leaf; forms neat geometric patterns when it is well established.
'Heron' One of many with a bird's foot leaf outline.
'Hibernica' The immensely vigorous Irish ivy, superb for large-scale ground cover.
'Ivalace' Dark green leaves with wavy margins.
'Parsley Crested' ('Cristata') Pale green leaves crimpled and crested at the margins.
'Sagittifolia' A large central lobe gives it a spearhead outline.
var. poetica The Italian ivy has amber yellow fruits instead of the usual black berries.

H. napalensis (*H. helix* var. *chrysocarpa*) The Himalayan ivy is also yellow fruited, and has narrow, often unlobed, glossy green leaves.

H. rhombea From Japan and Korea, with triangular green leaves on purple-flushed stems. It is generally seen in its variegated form, *H. rhombea* 'Variegata'.

HIBBERTIA Dilleniaceae

Evergreen climbers chiefly from Australia. Though tender, they will often spring again from ground level if cut down by frost. Generally they need greenhouse protection where frost is at all likely. Propagate from seed or from cuttings taken in summer.

H. dentata Clear yellow flowers in spring and summer.

H. scandens Showier than *H. dentata*, with a long succession of rich yellow, saucer-shaped flowers.

Holboellia coriacea

HOLBOELLIA Lardizabalaceae

Evergreen, twining climbers of vigorous growth, native to Asia. Can be raised from seed, layers or cuttings.

H. coriacea Purplish-white male flowers and slightly larger, greener female flowers in spring. The glossy, leathery foliage is attractive, but the flowers are barely visible. Fleshy, sausage-shaped purple fruits are occasionally produced.

H. latifolia Similar foliage and equally insignificant brownish or purplish-white flowers, deliciously fragrant and borne rather earlier than those of *H. coriacea*.

HOYA Asclepiadaceae

There are many species in this tropical genus, most twining or root-clinging climbers. Take cuttings in summer.

H. carnosa The justly popular wax flower, a greenhouse or house plant with thick, leathery, shiny green leaves

Ipomoea purpurea

and rounded clusters of waxy, palest pink flowers with a crimson eye; the flowers come in successive crops over two years or more. They are deliciously, even overpoweringly fragrant at night.

HUMULUS Cannabaceae

H. japonicus The Japanese hop is a perennial climber best grown from seed as an annual in cold climates. 'Variegatus' has foliage splashed with white.

H. lupulus The common hop, widespread in northern temperate zones and of great vigour. For gardeners rather than brewers the cultivar 'Aureus' is a handsome plant with lime yellow leaves that contrast spectacularly with deep green or purple-leaved shrubs. Divide or take basal cuttings in spring.

HYDRANGEA Hydrangeaceae

Most of the hydrangea species are shrubs; a few are root-climbers, with lacecap flower heads of central, fertile flowers surrounded by the showy, larger sterile ones. They are happiest in part shade. Layer or take cuttings in late summer.

Hydrangea petiolaris

H. anomala From the Himalayas and China, this has cream and white flowers in summer. The foliage is deciduous.

H. petiolaris (*H. anomala* subsp. *petiolaris*) From Japan, Korea and Taiwan. It is the most commonly grown climbing hydrangea, with flattish heads of white, lacy flowers in summer. It will cover a shady wall or tall tree trunk or stump, or form mounded ground cover. Deciduous.

H. serratifolia (*H. integerrima*) An evergreen species from Chile, with entire or sometimes toothed leaves (hence the apparently contradictory names) and frothy cream flowers in late summer.

IPOMOEA Convolvulaceae

A large genus of tropical plants including some spectacular climbers, evergreen and deciduous, of twining growth, needing warm conditions. Grow from seed.

I. alba (*I. bona-nox*, *I. noctiflora*, *Calonyction aculeatum*) This is the moonflower, with white, scented flowers opening in the evening.

I. coccinea (*Quamoclit coccinea*) With fragrant, vivid scarlet, yellow-throated flowers in late summer, this also has a yellow form, 'Luteola'.

I. indica (*I. acuminata*, *Pharbitis learii*) The blue dawn flower from tropical America has rich violet flowers, ageing to a pinker tone, in summer.

I. nil (*Pharbitis nil*) A tender perennial that can be grown as an annual to produce its purple, violet, red or blue flowers in one season. 'Scarlett O'Hara' has crimson flowers; double-flowered kinds are known as imperial Japanese morning glories.

I. purpurea (*Convolvulus purpurea*, *Pharbitis purpurea*) The common morning glory, annual or tender perennial with purple, violet or red-purple flowers; white, pink and double forms are also known.

I. quamoclit (*Quamoclit pennata*)
Feathery foliage and brilliant scarlet
flowers in summer and early autumn.
Annual.

I. tricolor Usually grown as an annual
to produce its broad, sky blue funnels,
nearly turquoise in the popular cultivar 'Heavenly Blue'.

JASMINUM Oleaceae

A large genus of twining and scrambling climbers (and some shrubs, not
listed here) from the Old World
tropics and subtropics. They need sun
to flower well; some are tender. Raise
from cuttings.

J. angulare From South Africa, this
needs conservatory treatment. The
dark green, evergreen foliage sets off
broad panicles of deliciously fragrant
white flowers in late summer.

J. azoricum Of similar tenderness, a
Madeiran plant with evergreen, trifoliate leaves and sweetly scented white
flowers opening from purple-flushed
buds in summer and on into winter.

J. beesianum From western China,
this is much hardier, an evergreen or
deciduous climber with small,
velvety-red or carmine flowers, the
exception in a genus of otherwise
white- or yellow-flowered species.
Like most of the white-flowered
kinds, it is fragrant.

J. dispermum A semi-evergreen or
deciduous Himalayan species with
fragrant white, pink-flushed flowers
in summer. For mild areas or a
conservatory.

J. floridum An evergreen or semi-
evergreen semi-climber from China,
with small but abundant yellow
flowers in summer.

J. mesnyi (*J. primulinum*) The primrose jasmine has soft yellow flowers
similar to, though larger than, those of
the winter jasmine; it is not as hardy,
and flowers in spring.

J. nudiflorum The winter jasmine is
so well known it needs no description,
and it is in any case hardly a climber.

J. officinale The common jasmine,
from the Himalaya and China and

*Jasminum
nudiflorum*

long cultivated in Europe for its exquisitely scented white flowers opening from pink buds. 'Affine' has slightly larger flowers; 'Aureum' or 'Aureo Variegatum' has leaves boldly variegated with bright yellow. There is also a rather dull, white-variegated form.

J. polyanthum Related to the common jasmine, but not as hardy. The strongly fragrant white flowers open from deep pink buds in late spring until late summer. The evergreen leaves are pinnate. China.

J. × stephanense A hybrid between the red-flowered *J. beesianum* and *J. officinale*. The result is a very vigorous, pink-flowered climber, fragrant, with leaves often variegated cream – but nicer when merely green.

J. simplicifolium* subsp. *suavissimum (*J. suavissimum*, *J. lineatum*) From Australia, this needs conservatory protection in cool climates; it bears its sweet-scented white flowers in late summer.

J. subhumile From the eastern Himalaya, Burma and China, evergreen, with glossy foliage and small, starry yellow, fragrant flowers that are borne in early summer.

KADSURA Schisandraceae

K. japonica From China, Japan and Taiwan, an evergreen twining climber with narrow, shiny, dark green foliage and fragrant cream flowers in summer, followed by scarlet fruits. Some shelter, and a lime-free soil, are needed for success. Take cuttings in late summer.

KENNEDIA Leguminosae

Another genus of Australian pea-flowered climbers for very mild areas or for the conservatory. All are easily raised from seed.

K. coccinea The coral pea has striking scarlet flowers in spring.

K. macrophylla Also has red flowers, borne in summer.

K. nigricans Of more sober colouring, chocolate and yellow, flowering in spring.

K. rubicunda Dusky red flowers in spring and early summer.

LABLAB Leguminosae

Lablab purpureus (*Dolichos lablab*) The hyacinth bean is a twining, tender perennial that can be grown from seed as an annual. Resembling the runner bean, it bears striking purple or white pea flowers in long racemes in summer. The pods and beans are both edible.

LAPAGERIA Philesiaceae

Named for the Empress Joséphine, Napoleon's first wife – née Joséphine de la Pagerie – this is a monotypic genus; the one species is an exquisite Chilean climber.

L. rosea This species has thin, twining stems set with heart-shaped, leathery, evergreen leaves. The flowers are narrow, elegant bells of waxy texture, rosy-crimson, white in the beautiful var. *albiflora*, or soft pink flecked with rose in the cultivar 'Nash Court'. Other named cultivars exist, but they are scarce and expensive. The type can be raised from fresh seed. Lapagerias ideally need deep, moist soil and warm shade; they are generally better suited to greenhouse cultivation where frost is at all likely.

Lapageria rosea var. *albiflora* (see page 81)

L. latifolius The everlasting pea is another perennial, more familiar than the last, with magenta-pink, pale pink or white flowers in summer. Scentless, but a fine plant; the white is especially lovely. It will climb or scramble, or flop down a bank.

L. magellanicus Given as a synonym for *L. nervosus* by many authors, though G. S. Thomas says, without describing it, that it is distinct.

L. nervosus Lord Anson's blue pea, a Chilean perennial with clear blue flowers, not large, but borne several to a stem, in summer. It is fragrant. For a long time rare, it may now be more easily obtainable as seed is offered commercially.

L. odoratus The sweet pea, an annual climber of which the innumerable modern cultivars can be had in a wide range of colours, on tall or dwarf plants. The species has fragrant purple flowers. Some of the older, intensely scented, named cultivars are now offered again: 'Matucana' and 'Quito' have magenta and purple flowers; 'Painted Lady' is an old rose-pink and white one.

LARDIZABALA Lardizabalaceae

A South American genus of evergreen climbers that need warm conditions, flourishing in Mediterranean regions.

L. biternata The foliage is composed of three to nine leathery, dark green leaflets. Chocolate-purple and white flowers appear in winter, the male flowers in long pendulous spikes and the female flowers singly. In warm climates fleshy, sausage-shaped purple fruits are produced; they are said to be good to eat.

LATHYRUS Leguminosae

A large genus of annuals and perennials, including the familiar annual sweet pea and scentless everlasting pea. Annuals and perennials alike can be raised from seed. Perennials can also be divided or raised from basal cuttings.

L. grandiflorus A perennial from southern Europe, with tuberous roots and scentless magenta-pink and purple flowers in summer.

Opposite:
Kennedia macrophylla (see page 81)

Right: *Lathyrus latifolius*

L. pubescens From Chile and Argentina, this is perennial, and less hardy than many. The flowers are lilac or lavender blue.

L. rotundifolius The Persian everlasting pea, a perennial with brick-pink flowers in summer.

L. sativus An annual pea with rather small flowers of pure turquoise blue.

L. tuberosus A perennial with creeping tuberous roots and clear pink flowers in summer. Europe and western Asia.

LITTONIA Liliaceae

L. modesta Very like a small gloriosa with nodding, cup-shaped, clear orange flowers. From Africa, it needs warm conditions and makes a charming pot plant. Propagated from division of tubers, offsets or sow seeds.

Lonicera giraldii

LONICERA Caprifoliaceae

There are many honeysuckles, some evergreen, some deciduous, and some – though not the most brightly coloured – deliciously fragrant. Most are hardy, though at least one species needs conservatory treatment in cold climates, and a large conservatory at that. All the climbing honeysuckles are twiners. Take cuttings in summer or autumn.

L. alseuosmoides An evergreen species from China that makes a thick growth of narrow leaves. Small yellow flowers, purple within, are rather lost in late summer.

L. × americana A hybrid between the European *L. caprifolium* and the Mediterranean *L. etrusca*. The child of the marriage is vigorous and free with its fragrant, white flowers which age through cream to deep yellow, purple-flushed outside. Mid summer.

L. × brownii This generally deciduous climber, dubbed the scarlet trumpet honeysuckle, has inherited many of the characteristics of its parent *L. sempervirens* from southern and eastern United States (the other parent is *L. hirsuta*, which is not described here). Bluish-green foliage sets off scarlet-orange flowers in showy whorls in late spring and again in late summer. Alas, they are scentless. Several cultivars have been named, of which 'Fuchsioides' is very like the type. 'Dropmore Scarlet' has an extremely long season.

L. caprifolium The early cream honeysuckle produces its powerfully fragrant cream flowers, just tinged with pink, in early summer. The glaucous leaves are perfoliate at the stem ends – uniting, that is, around the stem to form a cupped effect. This is one characteristic that distinguishes it from the common honeysuckle *L. periclymenum*.

L. etrusca From the Mediterranean, this is semi-evergreen, and relishes more sun than most honeysuckles, which generally like to have at least their roots in cool, shaded soil. Fragrant cream flowers, ageing to yellow, open among glaucous foliage in mid summer.

L. giraldii Forms dense growth of softly furry evergreen leaves, and produces its clusters of small red-purple flowers in mid summer. It is a little tender, being a native of southern China.

L. × heckrottii A second generation hybrid of *L. × americana* and *L. sempervirens*. It is almost more shrubby than twining. The brightest of the scented honeysuckles, 'Gold Flame', may be a cultivar of this hybrid or simply synonymous with it; the name describes the orange-pink and yellow flowers that are copiously borne from mid to late summer.

L. henryi Very like *L. alseuosmoides*, with broader leaves and yellow flowers flushed red-purple in summer.

L. hildebrandiana The giant honeysuckle is the one for which, unless you garden in a mild climate, you will need a large conservatory. An evergreen species from Burma, Thailand and south-western China, it has large leaves on tall, twining stems. The flowers, almost a hand's length in size, are fragrant and open creamy-white, ageing to warm yellow, during the summer.

L. implexa An evergreen climber of much more modest size than *L. hildebrandiana*, from the Mediterranean region, and reasonably hardy.

The foliage is glaucous beneath, the flowers yellow with a warm pink flush, appearing in summer.

L. japonica Not only Japanese but also Korean and Chinese, evergreen or semi-evergreen and extremely vigorous, producing a great tangle of growth and a long season of white, fragrant flowers that age to buff-yellow. 'Halliana' is a particularly good form. 'Aureo-reticulata' is popular with flower arrangers because of its brightly yellow-netted foliage; it is slightly tender and flowers only in hot seasons.

L. periclymenum The common honeysuckle is native to Europe and North Africa and has long been cultivated for its sweetly fragrant flowers, their scent carrying especially far at dawn and dusk. Two cultivars are commonly listed, but have perhaps become confused one with the other: 'Belgica', the early Dutch honeysuckle with pale yellow flowers stained purple-red outside, and the later, longer flowering 'Serotina' or late Dutch, the flowers deeper madder-purple, pinkish within.

L. sempervirens The trumpet honeysuckle, from the eastern United States, has received mention as the parent of some fine hybrids. It is itself a beautiful plant, with evergreen leaves and bright orange-scarlet trumpets in summer. 'Superba' is said to be an extra fine form; 'Sulphurea' has yellow flowers. Close to *L. sempervirens*, but accepted as a distinct species, is the yellow-flowered *L. flava*, the older flowers of which are flushed with orange.

L. similis var. **delavayi** Very like a modest-sized *L. japonica*, with fragrant white flowers ageing to yellow.

L. splendida From Spain, this has beautiful evergreen foliage, intensely glaucous-blue, and purple-red, fragrant flowers in summer. It needs shelter.

L. × tellmanniana A hybrid between *L. sempervirens* 'Superba' and *L. tragophylla*, a magnificent climber for half or even full shade, with long, coppery-orange trumpets in big clusters during the summer.

L. tragophylla From China, this is even more beautiful with very long, rich butter-yellow trumpets in summer, showing up to advantage in the shady conditions it prefers. It has no scent, but is spectacular enough not to need it.

Mitraria coccinea

MANDEVILLA Apocynaceae

Tender climbers from tropical South America. Sow seed or take summer cuttings.

M. splendens (*Dipladenia splendens*) Sometimes grown in greenhouses and makes a beautiful pot plant with its pink or carmine flowers. The twining stems can be cut back in late winter.

M. suaveolens The Chilean jasmine is in fact Argentinian not Chilean, and is not even a jasmine but a member of the periwinkle family. It is a beautiful twining climber with slender, heart-shaped leaves of a pretty, slightly bronzed green that set off shining white flowers of the characteristic propeller shape, though twice the size of the familiar blue periwinkle. The flowers appear from mid summer over a long season, and have a light perfume. Long, twinned seed pods follow, filled with silky fluff. The seeds germinate quickly and easily, but seedlings may take a long time to flower and some are inferior; a good form of *M. suaveolens* should be cherished and vegetatively propagated. Hardy on a sunny, sheltered wall even in quite cold areas.

MANETTIA Rubiaceae

M. bicolor A tender, evergreen, perennial, twining climber from South America, with tubular scarlet and yellow flowers of plushy texture over a long season from spring to autumn. Keep frost-free in winter. Take cuttings in summer.

Mandevilla suaveolens

MAURANDIA Scrophulariaceae

Central American plants in the fox-glove family, with flowers very like large foxgloves. Easily raised from seed to flower in their first year, but often hardier than expected, sprouting again from ground level if cut back by frost. All the climbing species have heart-shaped leaves.

M. barclaiana Purple flowers over a long season; white and pink forms also exist.

M. erubescens Rose-pink flowers.

MENISPERMUM Menispermaceae

The moonseed family also includes *Cocculus* and *Sinomenium*. Interesting rather than showy, they are quite attractive in fruit and mostly make vigorous growth, making them better suited to the outer reaches of the garden than to its choicer corners. Propagate from root cuttings, stem cuttings taken in summer or sow seed.

MINA Convolvulaceae

M. lobata From Mexico, this is a perennial twiner in a genus closely related to *Ipomoea*, but with tubular, curved flowers in place of the familiar morning glory shape. Opening crimson, they fade through orange to pale yellow and last throughout the summer. For sunny, sheltered places only, but easily raised from seed — started early enough, they will flower in their first season.

MITRARIA Gesneriaceae

M. coccinea A Chilean evergreen. Scarcely a climber, more of a scrambler, but — rather as ivy does — it will

Mina lobata

reach through other plants or cover the ground, though lacking the clinging roots of ivy. Small, dark green leaves set off the lopsidedly tubular, orange-scarlet, furry textured flowers. Propagate in summer from cuttings. For sheltered shade, a moist soil, and a mild climate.

MUEHLENBECKIA Polygonaceae

Southern hemisphere plants with slender stems and sparse foliage, rounded or violin-shaped, tiny insignificant flowers and whitish, translucent fruits. Take cuttings in summer.

M. axillaris From New Zealand, Australia and Tasmania, this is more of a creeper than a climber, forming a carpet of intertwining stems.

M. complexa A New Zealand species, very vigorous in mild areas, forming a copious tangle of black stems and rounded leaves, or noticeably violin-shaped in var. *trilobata*.

MUTISIA Compositae

A genus of climbing, woody daisies from South America, most not very easy to please but worth cossetting with rich soil and sun. Evergreen, they climb by leaf tendrils. The suckering stems of *Mutisia* species should not be dug up; both the potential new plants and the parent resent this treatment. Cuttings or seed should be tried if new stock is wanted.

M. clematis Tender, and spectacular when bearing its pendulous orange-scarlet daisy-like flowers in summer and early autumn. Given adequate shelter, or conservatory treatment in cold areas, it is one of the easiest to grow.

M. decurrens Not easy to establish; warm shade suits it best, and it is somewhat hardier than *M. clematis*. The elegant orange-scarlet daisies appear in summer.

M. ilicifolia Toothed, holly-like leaves and pink or mauve daisies in summer, or sporadically throughout the year. It has a regrettable tendency to be rather cluttered with dead brown leaves.

M. oligodon A trailer or climber with satiny, clear pink daisies in summer. It is about as hardy as *M. clematis*.

OXYPETALUM Asclepiadaceae

O. coeruleum (*Tweedia caerulea*) A South American twining perennial climber grown in greenhouses, or raised annually from seed to produce its fleshy sky-blue flowers among grey, hairy leaves. It is of modest growth.

PAEDERIA Rubiaceae

P. scandens A deciduous climber of Far Eastern origin, fairly vigorous, with twining stems set with dark green leaves (and a nasty smell when bruised). The tubular white flowers, purple-throated, are borne in clusters in late summer and are followed by orange fruits. Sun and shelter are needed. Take cuttings in late summer.

PANDOREA Bignoniaceae

P. jasminoides A twining evergreen from Australia, with the wide-mouthed funnels typical of its family, white or pink-flushed with a crimson-stained eye, in summer and autumn. It is of moderate vigour only, sometimes barely climbing, and needs a warm situation, or greenhouse protection. Propagate in summer from cuttings.

PARTHENOCISSUS Vitaceae

Unlike the closely related *Ampelopsis* and *Vitis*, the vines in this family may have little adhesive pads at the end of the leaf tendrils. Synonyms and confusions of naming proliferate among these three genera. Take cuttings in late summer.

P. henryana A beautiful and fairly vigorous deciduous climber with self-sticking tendrils and leaves with three or five leaflets, dark velvety green with a bronze flush and picked out in silvery-white and pink along the veins. It develops its best variegations when grown in shade. The autumn colour is deep crimson. A Chinese plant needing some shelter.

P. himalayana Less hardy than *P. henryana*, with lustrous green leaves dying off red in autumn. It is vigorous and more or less self-clinging.

P. inserta From the USA, this is also similar to the Virginia creeper, but with twining, not adhesive, tendrils. It has enough vigour to be used to disguise a shabby building or an ugly fence, and colours brightly in autumn.

P. quinquefolia The true Virginia creeper, an extremely vigorous self-clinging vine with five leaflets brilliantly coloured in flame and scarlet in autumn. Its common name indicates its origin: eastern USA.

P. thomsonii This Far Eastern species is close to *P. henryana*, with smaller leaves lacking the pretty veining. The young growths are madder-purple, the dying autumn foliage scarlet and crimson.

P. tricuspidata From the Far East, this is the Boston ivy, *not* the Virginia

Parthenocissus quinquefolia

creeper, though it is often so called. It has great vigour and is an efficient self-sticker with variably shaped leaves, simple, three-lobed or trifoliolate, turning to rich crimson in autumn. The cultivar 'Veitchii', with purple young foliage, is the original collection introduced by J. G. Veitch; 'Lowii' has smaller, more divided leaves described as 'crisped'.

PASSIFLORA Passifloraceae

The passion flowers are mostly native to Central and South America (a few to the Old World tropics). They were apparently given their name by Spanish priests in South America, who saw in the curiously structured flowers the symbols of the instruments of Christ's passion. The ten tepals represented ten apostles, the corona or ring of filaments within the tepals the crown of thorns, the five stamens the five wounds and the three stigmas the three nails.

Passion flowers are evergreen, more or less tender climbers with coiling tendrils each of which replaces a flower. The hardiest species will survive on a sunny sheltered wall even in quite cold areas, often springing freely from the base if cut down by frost; several make spectacular conservatory plants, or will grow out of doors in mild climates. Take cuttings in summer.

P. 'Allardii' A hybrid between the white form of *P. caerulea* 'Constance Elliott' and *P. quadrangularis*. It resembles the first parent and is nearly as hardy, with larger flowers, white tinged pink with a blue and white corona, in late summer and autumn

P. antioquiensis From Colombia, this belongs to the group of passion flowers formerly classed as *Tacsonia*, with long-tubed flowers. In this beautiful species they are rich red with a violet corona, and appear in late summer and autumn, though I have seen flowers in spring on a plant grown in a conservatory. It needs frost-free conditions.

P. caerulea The passion flower most familiar to gardeners in colder climates, this is a very vigorous climber with deep green, much divided leaves and white or barely blush-pink tepals surrounding the brightly coloured corona, which is zoned in purple, white and blue. They appear over a long season, though opening only in the sunshine, and are followed by orange, egg-shaped fruits. 'Constance Elliott' is a white-flowered cultivar.

P. × caerulea-racemosa A vigorous hybrid with violet-flushed flowers and purple corona. It is reasonably hardy, vigorous and free-flowering over a long season.

Opposite:
Parthenocissus tricuspidata in autumn tone (see page 89), mingling with variegated ivy

Passiflora antioquiensis

P. edulis The granadilla, producing the passion fruit familiar in greengrocers' shops. It is somewhat less hardy than the common *P. caerulea*, but even in cool maritime climates will occasionally ripen to produce fruit. The green-backed flowers are white, the corona formed of curly white, purple-banded filaments.

P. × exoniensis (*P. antioquiensis* × *P. mollissima*) For the mildest climates or conservatory only, it has great vigour and the rose-pink flowers are produced in abundance.

Passiflora × exoniensis

Pileostegia viburnoides

P. mollissima This has become some-thing of a weed in frost-free countries. It has long-tubed pink flowers.

P. racemosa Very vigorous when grown outside in a mild climate, but more restrained under glass. The flowers differ from those of other passion flowers in appearing in ter-minal racemes, not singly. Each is star-like, of rich scarlet with purple filaments.

P. umbilicata A *Tacsonia* (long-tubed passion flower) that is probably as hardy as *P. caerulea*, with smaller flowers richly coloured in amethyst or violet. It is of rapid and vigorous growth.

PERIPLOCA Asclepiadaceae

The silk vines get their name from the long, silky hairs attached to each seed; the seeds and their floss are packed in curious forked pods. Take cuttings in summer or sow seed.

P. graeca A deciduous, stem-twining climber from south-eastern Europe and western Turkey, with shiny dark green, oval leaves and clusters of slightly sticky, greenish-yellow flowers with purple-brown interiors, borne in summer. It is of fair vigour and easy to grow.

P. laevigata From the Canary Islands and North Africa, this is evergreen, less hardy, and barely climbs. The flowers are violet-brown within and appear over a long season from late spring to autumn.

P. sepium The Chinese silk vine, har-dier but of much more modest growth than *P. graeca*, which it resembles. The fragrant flowers are dark purple inside, and appear in clusters in mid summer.

PETRAEA Verbenaceae

A genus of shrubs and climbers from tropical America and the West Indies, of which one at least, *P. volubilis*, can be grown successfully under glass in colder climates. It is a fast-growing and vigorous twining climber with long trusses of deep violet, five-petalled flowers surrounded by the starry, pale lilac calyx. It may flower at more or less any season depending on temperature, and needs full sun, a rich soil and frost protection to succeed. Raise from summer cuttings.

PILEOSTEGIA Hydrangeaceae

P. viburnoides One of the small band of frost hardy, evergreen, root-clinging climbers. It grows slowly but will eventually cover a fair area with its leathery, deep green leaves, among which appear wide heads of tiny cream flowers in late summer and autumn. An Asian species, it needs a moist, rich soil to give of its best, and thrives in shade though flowering most freely with some sun. Propagate by layering or from late summer cuttings.

PLUMBAGO Plumbaginaceae

P. capensis The familiar, scrambling evergreen valued for its abundant sky-blue flowers over a long summer and autumn season. From South Africa, as its name implies, it scarcely stands frost but in mild climates will thrive in any reasonable soil. In colder areas it will, if permitted, fill a conservatory. Raise from seed or take cuttings in summer.

POLYGONUM Polygonaceae

In this large genus of (mainly) weeds are a few species that merit description here. They should perhaps now be referred to the genus *Fallopia*, but I retain the familiar name. Propagate from cuttings.

P. aubertii (*Fallopia aubertii, Bilder-dykia aubertii*) This is the plant generally grown as *P. baldschuanicum*, to which it is closely related, and known as mile-a-minute. Another name is Russian vine, though this species is from western China and Tibet and the true *P. baldschuanicum* is from southern USSR extending into Afghanistan and Pakistan. Both are extremely vigorous, twining climbers with heart-shaped leaves and sprays of tiny white or green-tinged flowers that turn pinkish in fruit; in the true *P. baldschuanicum* the slightly larger flowers may also be pink-tinted. Both species have a long summer season.

P. multiflorum From China and Taiwan, this is a half-woody, tuberous-rooted twining climber with dark, lustrous leaves on red stems, and sprays of little white flowers in summer. It is less hardy, and far less vigorous, than the other two species.

PUERARIA Leguminosae

P. lobata belongs to a genus allied to *Phaseolus*, which most gardeners know best as the haricot, runner or French bean. *Pueraria* has as its common name kudzu vine; this species is a perennial climber in mild areas or may be raised as an annual from seed to produce each year its long racemes of fragrant, purple-red pea flowers in summer. Perennials can also be divided. It is, however, a serious weed in the southern United States.

PYROSTEGIA Bignoniaceae

P. venusta Another of those spectacular, frost-tender, bignonia-type climbers, clinging by tendrils and making vigorous growth. The tubular flowers are rich orange in colour and appear in late winter and spring. Raise from summer cuttings. Native to Brazil.

RHODOCHITON Scrophulariaceae

R. atrosanguineum (*R. volubile*) An evergreen from Mexico, it climbs by means of twining leaf stalks. The heart-shaped leaves are rich green with purplish tints. The flowers are unique, each papery, muted magenta calyx formed like an umbrella or a coolie's hat, from which hangs a long-tubed, black-purple corolla, the tip expanding into five flared lobes. They appear over a very long season and are followed by balloon-like seed capsules; from the many seeds produced new plants can easily be raised to flower in their first year. In frost-free conditions the plant is a perennial.

*Pileostegia
viburnoides* (see
page 92)

ROSA Rosaceae

Of the enormous genus *Rosa*, several species and a good many hybrids and their cultivars are climbers, many of great beauty and often sweetly scented as well.

Roses 'climb' by means of hooked prickles; they are scramblers rather than true climbers, though some of the more vigorous will reach great heights once helped up to their first line of support. One may also distinguish between ramblers and climbers, though the two groups are now tend-

*Rhodochiton
atrosanguineum*
(see page 93)

ing to merge through the breeders' search for a large flowered, repeat flowering, hardy and scented climbing rose. For many of the older roses, however, the distinction remains a useful one, if only because it indicates the different pruning methods that should be used for the rose to give of its best. For the purposes of pruning, ramblers are the once-flowering roses, both wild species and their garden derivatives. They are pruned after flowering, by removing from the base all the old, weak wood – which may mean all the flowering stems, for many are of great vigour and will be throwing up strong new shoots from the base to replace those that are removed. Only if the rose can be expected to produce a crop of hips to give another season's display should some of the flowered branches be left. Climbers, which are generally of stiffer growth, bear large flowers of more formal aspect, and are generally repeat flowering. They are pruned in late winter, by occasionally removing some of the very oldest wood at the base, and principally by shortening the side shoots.

As with *Clematis*, so with *Rosa* – though with rather more diffidence – I take first a selection of climbing species and then an even more limited range of cultivars.

SPECIES

R. arvensis A native of Europe and Britain, this is a vigorous trailing rose flowering later than the dog rose, its creamy-white flowers sweetly scented. A parent of the Ayrshire roses – see 'Splendens'.

R. banksiae The Banksian rose from China is known in gardens by its double yellow and double white forms, though the wild type has single

The white-
flowered
Rosa filipes
'Kiftsgate'
photographed at
Kiftsgate Court,
Gloustershire (see
page 96)

flowers, of course, in white or yellow. The long, whippy, green stems are thornless; old wood bears flaky brown bark which is an attractive feature. The double white form 'Alba Plena' is scented like violets; the more commonly seen double yellow 'Lutea' has less fragrance.

All the Banksian roses produce their heads of many small flowers early in the year, in spring. Being less than totally frost hardy, they need a sheltered wall in cold climates, which presents difficulties of pruning and training, for the flowers are most abundantly borne on two- or three-year-old side shoots from long stems of five or more years' growth. The answer is to remove some shoots of five years or more each year, allowing the remainder to produce flowering side-shoots that can arch away from the wall. In milder climates the Banksian rose can be allowed to grow freely through a tree, where its graceful ways can be given rein.

R. bracteata The Macartney rose is another somewhat tender Chinese species of great beauty, with dark evergreen foliage and pure white flowers in leafy bracts; their whiteness is enhanced by the saffron-yellow stamens. They are lemon-scented.

R. brunonii The Himalayan musk rose, an extremely vigorous and prickly species with elegant foliage and scented white flowers. The finest cultivar known to us is 'La Mortola', with good-sized, pure white flowers.

R. *filipes* From western China, like *R. brunonii*, this belongs in the section Synstylae, a group of roses bearing a strong family resemblance. This one has become unquestionably the best-known because of 'Kiftsgate', which bears the characteristic immense wide heads of a hundred or more small, creamy-white, yellow-centred flowers after mid summer. Though often planted in small gardens it has no more place there than the equally abused weeping willow, for its vigour quickly makes it a menace. The original, in the eponymous garden in Gloucestershire, has filled more than one full-sized tree.

R. × *fortuniana* A hybrid of the Banksian rose with, perhaps, *R. laevigata*. It resembles the Banksian rose, with larger double white flowers, and needs a similar sunny wall in colder areas. It is sometimes incorrectly called *R. gentiliana*.

R. *gigantea* From south-western China, Burma and north-eastern India, this needs, as its native habitat implies, a warm and moist climate with mild winters. In suitable areas it is a vigorous climber with large leaves and huge single white flowers. It has lent its long petals and its fragrance to the old tea roses, as also some of its tenderness, and thus is a distant ancestor of the modern hybrid tea.

R. *helenae* Another of the Synstylae roses, a vigorous scrambler from China with hooked prickles and dark green foliage to set off rounded heads of small white flowers followed by tight bunches of little orange-red hips.

R. *laevigata* Though Chinese, this has so established itself in the United States that it is known as the Cherokee rose. It has shiny dark green, almost evergreen foliage and large, single, creamy-white flowers, very sweetly scented, early in the season. It is a little tender. See also *R. × anemonoides* and 'Ramona' under hybrid roses. (see page 102).

R. *longicuspis* One of the most beautiful of the Synstylae roses, a western Chinese species flowering after mid summer. Lustrous dark foliage sets off the great heads of creamy flowers with rich yellow centres and a powerful fragrance. The young shoots are mahogany red. It is very vigorous, though more restrained than 'Kiftsgate'.

R. *luciae* A glossy-leaved rambler from the Far East, closely related to the better-known *R. wichuraiana*.

R. *moschata* The musk rose is of uncertain origin, a large shrubby scrambler flowering late, with wide heads of creamy, musk-scented flowers among light green foliage.

R. *multiflora* An important parent of many ramblers, to which it has given its heads of many small flowers. *R. multiflora* itself has creamy flowers with a rich fragrance, and makes a thicket of arching stems. Little red hips follow the flowers. Forms of *R. multiflora* are used as stocks for budding; sometimes the scion has died to leave only the stock, forming a vigorous shrub. *R.* 'De la Grifferaie' is a coloured form, opening bright pink and fading to mauve. *R. multiflora platyphylla*, the seven sisters rose, is apparently so called because of the many colours in the flowers, vivid cerise on first opening, fading through lilac to near white: seven flowers in a truss will thus, it is said, be of seven different colours.

R. *rubus* The Synstylae group of roses dominates the climbing or scrambling species, numerically at least. This

Chinese species is another in the group, similar to *R. helenae* but of greater vigour, with rich cream flowers opening from pink-tinted buds; the petals are yellow at the base and the stamens are orange. The fragrance is like that of *R. multiflora*.

R. sempervirens Worthy of mention more as a parent of virtually evergreen climbers such as 'Adélaide d'Orléans' than in its own right, for it is not very fragrant. From southern Europe and North Africa, it is rather tender.

R. setigera This is the shrubby prairie rose of the eastern United States, also in section Synstylae; a parent of 'American Pillar'.

R. sinowilsonii From western China, it has been considered synonymous with *R. longicuspis*, but as grown in many gardens is distinct in its great beauty of foliage, glossy dark green above and mahogany red beneath, on red-brown stems. The white flowers are less noteworthy. It is not very hardy and needs a warm sheltered site.

R. wichuraiana From the Far East, this is a trailing, self-rooting evergreen with dark green foliage and small, fragrant white flowers in little mounded clusters in late summer. It is a parent of many ramblers. Its variegated form, *R. wichuraiana* 'Variegata', with leaves and shoots both more creamy-white and pink than green, is correspondingly lacking in vigour and would just about make a miniature rambler.

GARDEN HYBRIDS AND CULTIVARS

'Adélaide d'Orléans' A hybrid of *R. sempervirens*, with neat dark green foliage and hanging clusters of double, creamy-pink, scented flowers in mid summer. 1826.

'Aimée Vibert' A hybrid between a noisette and *R. sempervirens*, slightly tender, with lovely lustrous foliage and white, double flowers over a long, late-starting season (though earlier flowers are borne in mild areas where the unripened growths are not damaged by frost). 1828.

'Albéric Barbier' This vigorous rambler has the glossy foliage of its *R. wichuraiana* parentage, and clusters of creamy flowers opening from pointed, yellow buds over a long season. Apple-scented. 1900.

'Albertine' More of a big sprawly shrub, with shiny foliage and double, tawny pink flowers opening from coppery red buds; sweetly scented. Mid summer only. 1921.

'Alister Stella Gray' A tea-noisette rose with clusters of little, double, milk-white flowers opening from pointed yellow buds over a very long season. Sweetly scented. 1894.

'Aloha' A pillar rose rather than a genuine climber, with quite large, coral pink flowers of somewhat old-fashioned shape with a delectable perfume. 1949.

'American Pillar' The popularity of this vulgar, violent pink rambler defies comprehension. Single flowers by no means enhanced by their white eye; one season only, fortunately.

R. × **anemonoides** (*R. sinica* 'Anemone') A descendant of, and very like, *R. laevigata*, but tougher, with elegant wide single flowers of clear pink over a long season. c. 1895. See also 'Ramona'.

'Blush Rambler' An old *R. multiflora* rambler with pale pink, semi-double flowers, very fragrant. Vigorous and nearly thornless. 1903.

Opposite:
'Albertine' (see page 97)

'New Dawn' (see page 101)

'**Bobbie James**' A tremendous Synstylae rambler with big heads of creamy white, nearly single flowers, yellow-centred, filling the surrounding air with their rich perfume in its summer season. 1960.

'**Cécile Brunner, Climbing**' ('Climbing Bloomfield Abundance') A vigorous climber bearing copious quantities – though barely repeating – of little clear pink hybrid tea flowers, each one no bigger than the top joint of a finger. Fragrant. 1894.

'**Céline Forestier**' A tea-noisette with creamy yellow flowers, touched with apricot, of flat-faced, quartered shape. Tea-scented and very perpetual. 1842.

'**Chaplin's Pink Climber**' This is 'American Pillar' × 'Paul's Scarlet', with the brashness that parentage suggests. Strong pink, semi-double flowers borne on vigorous rambling growth. 1928.

'**Claire Jacquier**' Another tea-noisette, like a tougher and much more vigorous 'Alister Stella Gray', the pretty, warm yellow, fragrant flowers borne mainly in mid summer. 1888.

'**Cooper's Burmese Rose**' As known in cultivation, this seems to be a hybrid between *R. gigantea* and *R. laevigata*, which it resembles. Lustrous foliage and single, pure white flowers. It is somewhat tender.

'**Crimson Shower**' Its other name, 'Red Dorothy Perkins', indicates something of its appearance: crimson, double flowers, which open late and have a long flowering season. A vigorous rambler, but lacking scent. 1951.

'**Cupid**' A thorny climber with single hybrid tea flowers of clear peach-pink, fragrant, followed by large red hips. 1915.

'**Debutante**' A fine, pure pink double rambler derived from a pink hybrid perpetual and *R. wichuraiana*. 1902.

'**Dorothy Perkins**' An Edwardian rambler with almost scentless, hard pink flowers. There are better things about now, 'Debutante' for one. 1901.

'**Duchesse d'Auerstädt**' A noisette of great quality, with rich yellow double flowers in the style of 'Gloire de Dijon'. For anyone blessed with

plenty of wall space there could be few lovelier things to collect than the noisette and tea-noisette roses, with their beautiful colouring and rich perfume. 1888.

'Easlea's Golden Rambler' Despite its name, this is a climber with large rich yellow flowers opening from red-stained buds, among fine glossy foliage. Once flowering, richly fragrant. 1932.

'Emily Gray' A rambler with lustrous foliage and buff-yellow, semi-double flowers of good size, sweetly scented, in mid summer. Vigorous. 1918.

'Etoile de Hollande, Climbing' In an arbitrary selection many good roses must be omitted, but of several old crimson-red climbers with the expected rich, velvety scent, this is indispensable. Vigorous and recurrent. 1919.

'Félicité et Perpétue' A late-flowering and nearly evergreen *R. sempervirens* hybrid, very hardy and vigorous, with, clusters of creamy-white rosette-shaped flowers, borne after mid summer. 1827.

'Francis E. Lester' A rambler of vigorous, bushy growth with clusters of blush to white single, yellow-eyed flowers with rich fruity scent; mid summer. 1946.

'François Juranville' A rambler with coral pink, flat, double flowers, almost as large as those of 'Albéric Barbier', and a similar apple scent. Vigorous and prickly. 1906.

'Gloire de Dijon' A beautiful and famous tea-noisette constantly in flower, with richly fragrant, buff-yellow, peach-shaded blooms. Inclined to be leggy. 1853.

'Golden Showers' More of a pillar rose than a climber, with shiny foliage and large, double, light yellow, fragrant flowers. Recurrent. 1956.

'Goldfinch' A rambler with clusters of little, semi-double flowers opening from warm yellow buds and fading to near white; fruity *R. multiflora* scent and just one season of flower. 1907.

'Guinée' A deep black-crimson, large flowered climber with the expected rich perfume; somewhat recurrent. 1938.

'Handel' A climber with large double flowers opening from pointed buds, creamy-white with deep pink edging. 1965.

'Kew Rambler' A hybrid of the half-shrubby, half scrambling *R. soulieana* and 'Hiawatha', a scentless rose with crimson, white-eyed flowers. It has from the first parent, greyish foliage and from the second, single rose pink flowers with a white centre. A vigorous rambler with a rich, fruity scent. 1912.

'Lady Hillingdon, Climbing' The climbing sport of an old, hardy tea rose, with exquisite pointed buds opening to loosely double flowers of warm apricot yellow; plum-maroon young growths. Scented, vigorous, and perpetually in flower; a rose to treasure. 1917.

'Lawrence Johnston' ('Hidcote Yellow') A richly scented, richly coloured yellow climber of vigorous growth and a long season of bloom. 1923.

'Leverkusen' Glossy, light green foliage and lemon-yellow, lemon-scented flowers in mid summer and later, on branching, semi-shrubby growth. 1954.

Madame Alfred Carrière' A vigorous climber of noisette descent with light green foliage and large, double, blush-white flowers, fragrant and recurrent. Will grow and flower on a north wall. 1879.

'Madame Butterfly, Climbing' The climbing sport of a famous old hybrid tea, itself a sport of 'Ophelia'. Elegant flowers of pale pink, with a repeat season. 1918.

'Madame Caroline Testout, Climbing' Scarcely scented, but valued for its abundant, cool pink flowers on tall stems. Recurrent. 1890.

'Madame Grégoire Staechelin' ('Spanish Beauty') One season only, in early summer, of large, semi-double pink flowers delightfully scented of sweet peas. Vigorous growth. 1927.

'Maigold' A newish rose, half shrub and half climber, with vicious prickles and semi-double, orange-stained yellow flowers over a long season; fine, lustrous leaves. 1953.

'Maréchal Niel' A tea rose to treasure in a greenhouse or conservatory, or outside in warm gardens, with nodding flowers of gentle yellow. 1864.

'Meg' One parent was 'Madame Butterfly', from which this newish, vigorous and bushy climber has its large, single or semi-double apricot-pink flowers mostly borne in one crop. 1954.

'Mermaid' A famous hybrid of *R. bracteata*, and apt to suffer in cold winters, with glossy near-evergreen foliage and wide, single, clear yellow flowers enhanced by amber stamens which remain decorative after the petals fall. Fragrant and with a long season. 1918.

'New Dawn' Virtually a perpetual-flowering rambler, with small but formally shaped flowers of clear pale pink among shiny green leaves. Sweetly scented. 1930.

'Ophelia, Climbing' Paler than 'Madame Butterfly', but of equally beautiful formal hybrid tea shape, the fragrant, pale pink flowers borne over a long season. 1912.

'Paul's Himalayan Musk' A vigorous rambler with clusters of many small, double, lilac-pink, fragrant flowers in mid summer. For garden effect this is a pink-flowered equivalent of 'Rambling Rector' and the like.

'Paul's Lemon Pillar' From the same stable, but of entirely different character from the last, this is a climber with a single crop of very large, beautifully formed hybrid tea blooms, lemon-white in colour and very sweetly scented. 1915.

'Paul's Scarlet' Often seen, this crimson-scarlet climber has flowers of informal shape borne chiefly in mid summer. Vigorous growth, little scent. 1916.

'Pink Perpétue' A newish rose suitable for a pillar, with a long season of double, bright pink flowers, fragrant. 1965.

'Polyantha Grandiflora' The name is not valid, but it is recognized by gardeners as describing a vigorous rambler of the Synstylae section with glossy foliage and big heads of fragrant white flowers followed by small, orange-red hips. 1886.

'Pompon de Paris, Climbing' A miniature doll's house climber with small, deep pink rosettes and tiny leaves.

'Pink Perpétue'
(see page 101)

'Rambling Rector' A very vigorous Synstylae rambler with wide heads of creamy-white, small, semidouble flowers in mid summer, with a powerful, far-reaching fragrance. Perhaps the same as 'Shakespeare's Musk'.

'Ramona' A deeper coloured sport of *R. × anemonoides*, each wide single flower of rich carmine pink with silvery-buff reverse. 1913.

'Réveil Dijonnais' A brilliantly coloured, vigorous and bushy climber with semi-double or near-single flowers, scarlet with yellow centre and reverse, mostly borne in mid summer. Agreeable scent. 1931.

'Rose-Marie Viaud' One of the few violet-mauve ramblers (others are 'Bleu Magenta', 'Violette' and 'Veil-chenblau') with clusters of little double flowers opening bright pink and quickly fading to lilac and mauve; one late season. Vigorous and nearly thornless. 1924.

'Sander's White' A popular white rambler on account of its delightful scent, otherwise somewhat like a white 'Dorothy Perkins' and of similar vigour. 1912.

'Shot Silk, Climbing' The climbing sport of a wonderful old hybrid tea with salmon pink, fragrant flowers; recurrent. 1924.

'The Garland' A hybrid of *R. moschata* and *R. multiflora*, with the expected vigour and rich, fruity perfume from abundant, small, semidouble, flat flowers with quilled petals, cream from salmon buds, in mid summer. 1835.

'Veilchenblau' Another of the lilac-flowered ramblers, and the only one with much scent from its little, semi-double flowers borne in clusters on almost thornless stems. It flowers ahead of 'Rose-Marie Viaud', in mid summer. 1909.

'Violette' Not unlike 'Veilchenblau', flowering just a little later and ageing to a greyer tone of mauve. Little scent. 1921.

'Wedding Day' Derived from *R. sinowilsonii*, with good foliage and large clusters of single white flowers opening from yellow buds. Apt to become stained with pink with age, forming a less happy contrast with the yolk-yellow stamens. Very fragrant and vigorous. 1950.

'William Allen Richardson' The richest in colour of the noisettes, at least in bud and at first opening, deep orange-yellow fast fading to off-white in sun. Maroon young growths. If only it retained its colour it would be worth wall space despite the rather shapeless flowers. 1878.

RUBUS Rosaceae

The large bramble family includes some interesting and decorative scramblers valued chiefly for their foliage. Easy to increase by division or tip layering. All the species described below are from China.

R. flagelliflorus An evergreen climber, with handsome foliage, buff-felted beneath. The stems are clad only in minute prickles.

'Sander's White'

R. henryi Also evergreen, with striking, deep green, lustrous, three-lobed leaves borne on long stems. Variety *bambusarum* is more elegant in leaf, the foliage in three distinct leaflets.

R. ichangensis A recent reintroduction from China, an attractive semi-evergreen species with large, leathery leaves tapering to a point. The fruits are said to be of good flavour. For sheltered gardens only.

R. lambertianus Scandent, prickly stems and shining green leaves, very variable in shape.

R. parkeri A deciduous species with slender stems; the wavy-edged, long-pointed leaves are russet-felted beneath.

SANDERSONIA Liliaceae

S. aurantiaca From South Africa, this is much like a small gloriosa in general aspect, but for its flowers, which are tubby urns of light tangerine. Need-

Senecio macroglossus

ing frost protection, it adapts well to pot culture. Propagate as for gloriosa (see page 76).

SCHISANDRA Schisandraceae

Twining shrubs, both deciduous and evergreen; the species in cultivation are from Asia, with dioecious flowers (male and female on separate plants). They grow well in humus-rich soil in a partly shaded position and can be raised from late-summer cuttings.

S. chinensis A tall species with fragrant, white or blush flowers in late spring. Female plants bear striking scarlet fruits if given a partner.

S. propinqua A low-altitude, evergreen Himalayan species needing protection from frost. The Chinese var. *chinensis* (var. *sinensis*) is hardier, and bears its terracotta and lime flowers in late summer and autumn.

S. rubriflora (*S. grandiflora* var. *rubriflora*) A deciduous climber, less vigorous than the last, which bears blood-red fragrant flowers in late spring and early summer. Scarlet berries follow, borne in hanging spikes.

S. sphenanthera A deciduous plant with similarly coloured flowers to those of *S. propinqua*, but borne in late spring; in general aspect it resembles *S. grandiflora*.

SCHIZOPHRAGMA Hydrangaceae

More climbing hydrangeas, self-clinging by aerial roots, and like *Hydrangea petiolaris* happy in shade though flowering best in sun. They are slow to make much growth but in time become tall. Like those of hydrangeas, the flowers are composed of small, insignificant fertile flowers surrounded by large showy bracts, giving a lacecap effect rather bolder in this genus than in *Hydrangea*. Propagate from layers or late-summer cuttings.

S. hydrangeoides A tall, deciduous climber with toothed leaves and wide, cream-bracted flowerheads in summer. It is a native of Japan. In 'Roseum' the bracts are flushed with pink.

S. integrifolium This has larger flowerheads and bolder, long-lasting bracts, of rich cream colouring. From China, where it grows in cool moist valleys up rocky cliffs.

SEMELE Liliaceae

Like *Ruscus*, the butcher's broom, to which it is closely related, *Semele* has flattened stems or cladodes performing the function of leaves; the tiny flowers are borne in the middle of the cladodes.

S. androgyna From the Canary Islands, this is in effect a vigorous climbing butcher's broom with evergreen stems and large cladodes, making it a handsome if potentially rampant plant. The flowers are greenish-yellow.

SENECIO Compositae

The huge genus *Senecio*, which includes such garden undesirables as ragwort and groundsel, offers some ornamental species of high value. Among them are a few climbers, some tender and one, at least, a valuable hardy garden scrambler. Raise from seed or summer cuttings.

S. confusus The Mexican flame vine, a vigorous if tender stem-twiner, with orange daisies in summer.

S. macroglossus A South African species grown as a house plant in cold climates for its ivy-shaped, dark green, lustrous leaves. It has yellow flowers.

S. scandens Fairly hardy and moderately vigorous, scrambling through any convenient supporting shrub to produce, among fresh light green leaves, massed small lemon-yellow daisies in autumn. It has a wide distribution in the wild in eastern Asia, and is a much more effective garden plant than its description suggests.

S. tamoides A tender African species producing, among rather fleshy, glaucous leaves, copious bright yellow daisies in winter if given a moderate amount of warmth.

SINOFRANCHETIA
Lardizabalaceae

S. chinensis A vigorous, deciduous, twining climber with trifoliate leaves, glaucous beneath. Small white flowers are borne in May and are followed, on female plants, by attractive grape-like purple fruits. a male pollinator does not seem to be necessary of these fruits to be set.

SMILAX Liliaceae

Many species of prickly stemmed tendril climbers, both deciduous and evergreen, with a few non-climbers, form this large genus. They are apt to form tangled thickets and some have handsome foliage. Increase by division or from seed.

S. aspera A rather tender evergreen from the Mediterranean area, the Canary Islands and Asia, with glossy, leathery leaves varying from heart-shaped to lanceolate. Little fragrant, pale-green flowers in late summer may in suitable climates be followed by red fruits.

S. china The China root from which a specific against gout was once obtained. It is a deciduous scrambler with variably shaped leaves sometimes colouring in autumn. The lime-green flowers appear in late spring and are followed by red berries.

S. discotis A deciduous climber from China, this one bearing black fruits.

S. excelsa A handsome evergreen climber, tall and vigorous, with pointed evergreen leaves and red berries. From eastern Europe and western Asia, it is probably hardier than the last three, though less so than *S. rotundifolia*.

S. rotundifolia From eastern North America, this deciduous climber has heart-shaped leaves, shiny on both surfaces, and black, white-bloomed fruits. It is of more modest growth than *S. excelsa*.

SOLANUM Solanaceae

This enormous and widespread genus, the nightshades, includes some garden climbers of the greatest beauty for temperate climates. They require full sun, but are not fussy about soil. Increase from cuttings taken in late summer.

S. crispum A fast-growing, half-shrubby, semi-evergreen scrambler with potato-like flowers of rich violet enhanced by the cone-like cluster of bright yellow stamens. The cultivar 'Glasnevin' ('Autumnale') flowers over a long summer and autumn season.

S. jasminoides A semi-evergreen climber with slender twining stems and thin-textured leaves with the typical sour Solanaceae smell when bruised. The flowers are milky or slate-blue and borne over a very long season. In 'Album' they are pure white, with the bright yellow cone of stamens the more telling as a result. Coming from further north than the Chilean *S. crispum*, *S. jasminoides* from Brazil is correspondingly rather less frost-resistant, generally requiring cool greenhouse treatment in frost-prone areas.

S. valdiviense Though native to Chile and Argentina, this is possibly less hardy still. It is half-climbing, with fragrant mauve or white flowers in late spring.

The ripening fruits of *Schisandra rubriflora* (see page 104)

Opposite: *Schizophragma hydrangeoides* (see page 105)

Left: *Solanum crispum*

SOLLYA Pittosporaceae

Delightful, frost-tender, slender-stemmed, twining evergreen plants easily raised from seed or cuttings, both native to Australia.

S. heterophylla The bluebell creeper has cerulean blue bells in summer and autumn.

S. parviflora (*S. drummondii*) Linear leaves and smaller, darker blue flowers.

STAUNTONIA Lardizabalaceae

S. hexaphylla A vigorous twining evergreen very like *Holboellia*, with large, leathery, dark green leaves and fragrant, mauve-flushed white flowers in spring. In suitable climates, with long hot summers, this Far Eastern native may produce its egg-shaped purple fruits, said to be edible but insipid. Raise from seed or late-summer cuttings.

STREPTOSOLEN Solanaceae

The large Solanaceae family contains many good plants, mostly rather frost-tender.

S. jamesonii The marmalade bush will stand scarcely any frost but makes a pretty pot plant. Of scrambling habit, it has rich green leaves to set off the abundant, bright orange, flared trumpets borne in clusters in late spring and summer. Increase from cuttings.

TECOMARIA Bignoniaceae

T. capensis The Cape honeysuckle from South Africa, a fairly vigorous, self-clinging and twining climber with pinnate leaves and brilliant scarlet trumpets in terminal spikes, their

season depending on climate. In cold areas this is a spectacular conservatory plant; in milder gardens a position on a warm, sunny wall is suitable, and flowers will be produced in late summer and autumn.

THLADIANTHA Cucurbitaceae

T. dubia This is a Chinese species, a tendril climber with herbaceous growths springing each year from a tuberous root. Bell-shaped flowers, bright yellow in colour, are borne in summer. Raise from seed or take basal cuttings in spring. The plant is resistant to a few degrees of frost.

THUNBERGIA Acanthaceae

T. alata The familiar black-eyed Susan, a tender annual climber from tropical Africa with five-petalled flowers, orange, yellow or cream, with a black-purple centre. Grow from seed. Often grown as a pot plant.

TRACHELOSPERMUM Apocynaceae

These jasmine-like climbers belong to the periwinkle family, as the shape of their sweetly fragrant flowers testifies. They are self-clinging and twining evergreens needing at least half-sun, and a sheltered position in colder gardens. Propagate from layers or summer cuttings.

T. asiaticum (*T. divaricatum*, *T. crocostemon*) From Japan and Korea, densely leafy, with glossy dark green foliage and creamy-white flowers ageing to Naples yellow, borne in late summer.

T. jasminoides Larger in leaf than *T. asiaticum* and rather less frost resistant, with less efficient aerial roots. The flowers are also larger, white ageing to cream and intensely fragrant. This Chinese species has a fine variegated form, 'Variegata', which is apparently hardier than the green-leaved kind; the foliage is edged and splashed with cream and often turns to crimson-pink in winter.

T. majus From Japan, this is apparently regarded by botanists as a variant of *T. asiaticum*. There is a different plant in cultivation under this name: it is a vigorous plant, taller and larger in leaf than the other species. The winter foliage often turns red.

TRIPTERYGIUM Celastraceae

Scarcely known, these deciduous scrambling shrubs are best suited to larger gardens. They are east Asian in origin and will grow in most humus-rich soils. Increase from late summer cuttings or from seed.

T. regelii Quite handsome foliage, and big sprays of little, greeny-white flowers in late summer followed by three-winged, pale green fruits.

T. wilfordii Similar to *T. regelii*, but with red-purple fruits.

TROPAEOLUM Tropaeolaceae

After the common nasturtium, the best-known member of this genus from Central and South America is probably the Scottish flame flower; but it also includes many other desirable annual and perennial trailing or climbing plants; the true climbers attach themselves by twisting leaf stalks. Most prefer full sun; the Scottish flame flower, exceptionally, needs cool conditions and a moist, preferably acid soil.

T. azureum None too easy to grow, but seed can now be obtained for the adventurous gardener to attempt to raise this charming, frail climber with – exceptionally in the genus – violet-blue flowers. Like most of the genus it is a native of Chile (others extend up the South American continent to Mexico), but unlike many Chilean plants it does not adapt well to European conditions and should be given greenhouse treatment, the little tubers re-potted each year in autumn and kept in some warmth to flower from late winter.

T. majus The common nasturtium, of which some forms are energetic interweavers with tall, virtually climbing stems. Easily raised from seed.

Tropaeolum majus,
a double-flowered
cultivar

*Tropaeolum
tuberosum*

it is not easy to establish, once settled it may smother its neighbours.

T. speciosum The Scottish flame flower, well known for its dainty, fresh green foliage and bright scarlet flowers, which appear in late summer and are seen to best effect against a dark background. The frail stems die down each year to fleshy roots, from which new plants can be raised by chopping them up into sections each bearing a growth point. New plants can also be grown from the bright blue fruits. Although it is said to need an acid soil, it may also thrive in other soils such as limey clay.

T. tricolorum Produces its small frail stems and little leaves from tuberous roots. The flowers are like red and black fishes, the calyx and spur scarlet, the lobes tipped with black.

T. tuberosum A much more muscular plant, with broad, rounded, lobed leaves and quite large orange and yellow flowers. Early-flowering forms should be sought for cold gardens, lest the flowers fail to open before they are caught by autumn frosts; one such form is 'Ken Aslet'. The specific name alludes to the fat, abundant tubers, which are edible. Each season they multiply so as to pile up on one another out of the ground; the uppermost can be easily detached and kept frost-free for replanting the following spring, while those left in the ground may be protected by peat or grit.

VITIS Vitaceae

This genus of deciduous tendril climbers includes the common grape vine as well as many very ornamental species. They are of easy culture and, mainly, vigorous growth. Best raised from eye cuttings taken in winter.

T. peregrinum The Canary creeper, but despite its name a native of Peru. An annual climber, it has pale foliage and bright yellow flowers in summer, ideal for adding another season of interest to a shrub that performs earlier or later in the year. Raise from seed.

T. polyphyllum Always sought after for its bright glaucous-blue foliage and rich yellow flowers. Like many mat-forming plants, it can be encouraged to weave its long stems through neighbouring plants. Though

V. amurensis From eastern Asia, it resembles the grape vine, with lobed leaves colouring richly to plum and crimson in autumn.

V. 'Brant' A complex hybrid of the grape vine, *V. vinifera*, which it resembles, bearing sweet black grapes. The autumn colour is bronze-purple set off by green veins.

V. coignetiae Extremely vigorous, with great rounded leaves turning scarlet, flame and blood red in autumn. It is a Japanese species and by no means as easy to propagate as most vines, but well worth accommodating in a large tree or to decorate a wall where space allows.

V. davidii A Chinese vine, easily recognizable by its spiny stems. The heart-shaped leaves are dark, lustrous green above and often turn to rich red in the autumn. The small black grapes are edible.

V. flexuosa An elegant vine of restrained growth, with shiny green, heart-shaped leaves. It is usually represented in gardens by var. *parvifolia* from the Himalayas, which has smaller leaves, bronzed above and purple beneath when young.

Autumn tints the large leaves of *Vitis coignetiae*

V. labrusca The first, alphabetically, of the North American vines, known as the fox grape. Of great vigour, it has woolly young shoots and dark green leaves, white beneath. The black grapes are said to have a musky flavour, and this species has been used in breeding many cultivated American grapes.

V. pulchra (*V. flexuosa major*) Possibly a hybrid between *V. amurensis* and *V. coignetiae*. It is very vigorous, with heart-shaped, slightly lobed leaves turning blood red and flame in autumn.

V. riparia The river bank grape of North America, a vigorous species with broadly heart-shaped, lobed and toothed leaves, glossy green on both surfaces. The flowers are mignonette-scented though, like all vitis flowers, of little beauty, and are followed by black grapes.

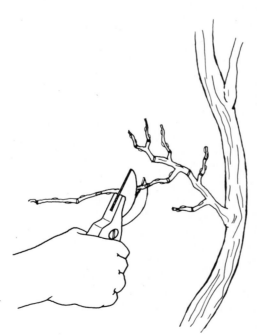

Winter pruning of wisteria: the laterals are cut back to two or three buds

V. vinifera The common grape vine, perhaps originally from Asia Minor but for long widespread in cultivation; there are now hundreds of cultivars developed for their fruiting and vineyard qualities. There are also some very ornamental kinds with handsome foliage. Among these are:
'Apiifolia' The parsley vine, with deeply cut and divided leaves;
'Fragola' The strawberry vine, so called from the flavour of its fruits;
'Incana' The dusty miller vine, the grey-green leaves white with cobwebby felt;
'Purpurea' The Teinturier grape, the young shoots downy-white soon turning claret-purple, wonderful with grey-foliaged plants or to accompany flowers of subfusc mauve and pink colouring.

WATTAKAKA Asclepiadaceae

W. sinensis (*Dregea sinensis*) A charming twining climber with hoya-like, scented white flowers with a central zone of red flecks, borne in clusters in summer. The leaves are grey-felty beneath. Formerly difficult to obtain, it is now offered by a few nurseries and is well worthy of space on a sheltered wall, or in cold areas in a conservatory. Propagate from cuttings taken in late summer or raise from seed.

WISTERIA Leguminosae

Beautiful, often sweetly fragrant, twining climbers with deciduous pinnate leaves and long racemes of pea-flowers in early summer. Wisterias can be spectacular, and can also be disappointing when, if not correctly pruned, they make masses of luxuriant foliage and little or no flower. Too rich a soil, or too little sun, can also contribute to this undesirable state.

Pruning should be carried out in two stages: in summer the long laterals are cut back to about 15 cm (6 in) and in mid winter these are shortened again, back to two or three buds. Wisteria can be propagated successfully by layering or from cuttings taken in summer. Wall-grown plants in particular need this twice-yearly attention; wisterias can also be grown on pergolas, or similar structures, or into tall trees.

W. floribunda The Japanese wisteria has fragrant, violet-blue flowers borne in late spring and early summer. Several cultivars are in cultivation, including one with white flowers ('Alba'), and with rose-pink flowers ('Rosea'), and the double-flowered 'Violacea Plena'. Perhaps the most spectacular is forma *macrobotrys*, with blue-lilac flowers in yard-long racemes, or even longer. It needs to be grown on a support which will allow these long tresses to hang free to look its best. It is therefore an ideal plant for a pergola or trained against a large wall.

W. ×formosa A hybrid between *W. sinensis* and *W. floribunda* 'Alba'; the result is a plant much like the first parent. Here belongs the cultivar 'Issai' with short tresses of lilac-blue flowers.

W. frutescens An uncommon and less attractive species from North America, bearing its mauve, yellow-eyed, fragrant flowers in short, crowded trusses in summer.

W. macrostachys Similar to *W. frutescens*, with longer racemes of lilac-purple flowers in early summer. It too is from North America.

W. sinensis The wisteria most commonly seen. It is distinguished from *W. floribunda* by its anti-clockwise-twining stems – the Japanese species twines clockwise. The Chinese *W. sinensis* bears pale to deep mauve-lilac, fragrant flowers in trusses longer than those of typical *W. floribunda*, in late spring, and sometimes again in high summer. Garden cultivars include the white 'Alba', and double-flowered 'Black Dragon' and 'Plena'. A form named 'Prolific' flowers especially freely.

W. venusta Though scarcely scented by comparison with the deliciously sweet *W. sinensis*, this is a very beautiful Japanese species, less vigorous than the Chinese wisteria, with large white flowers in short racemes in early summer. This white form is in fact a Japanese garden plant; the wild species, forma *violacea*, has violet flowers.

Climbers for Selected Sites and Qualities

CLIMBERS FOR SOUTH- OR WEST-FACING ASPECTS

Actinidia deliciosa
A. kolomikta
Campsis radicans
C. × tagliabuana
Clematis alpina
C. armandii
C. chrysocoma var. *sericea*
C. cirrhosa
C. cirrhosa var. *balearica*
C. florida 'Sieboldii'
C. macropetala
C. montana
C. tangutica
C. tibetana subsp. *vernayi* 'Orange Peel'

Jasminum officinale
†*J. polyanthum*
Lonicera etrusca
L. giraldii
L. henryi
L. japonica 'Halliana'
L. periclymenum
†*Passiflora caerulea*
Rosa (many)
Solanum crispum 'Glasnevin'
†*S. jasminoides*
Schizophragma hydrangeoides
Vitis vinifera
Wisteria (all)

CLIMBERS FOR NORTH- OR EAST-FACING ASPECTS

Akebia quinata
†*Berberidopsis corallina*
Berchemia racemosa
Celastrus orbiculatus
Clematis alpina
C. macropetala
C. montana
Clematis (many large flowered cultivars)
Hedera (most)
Hydrangea anomala
H. petiolaris
H. serratifolia

Lonicera × americana
L. caprifolium
L. periclymenum
L. × tellmanniana
L. tragophylla
†*Muehlenbeckia complexa*
Parthenocissus (all)
Pileostegia viburnoides
Rosa (many, e.g. 'Madame Alfred Carrière')
Schizophragma hydrangeoides
S. integrifolium
Vitis coignetiae

* plants which will only grow well outside in a frost-free climate; elsewhere should be grown in a cold greenhouse or conservatory
† plants tolerant of some frost if given a sheltered position or grown in mild conditions; otherwise these need the protection of a conservatory

Opposite: *Vitis vinifera* 'Purpurea' (see page 112)

CLIMBERS FOR RESTRICTED SPACES

Aconitum volubile
Adlumia fungosa
*Anredera cordifolia
†*Asteranthera ovata*
*Billardiera
*Bomarea
*Cardiospermum
Clematis texensis (and hybrids, and some others)
Codonopsis
†*Eccremocarpus scaber*
Euonymus fortunei var. *radicans*
†*Hedera helix* cvs. (some)
*Ipomoea

†*Kadsura japonica*
*Lablab purpureus
*Lapageria rosea
Lathyrus
†*Mina lobata*
†*Mutisia*
*Oxypetalum
Rosa (some)
†*Solanum*
†*Sollya*
†*Thladiantha dubia*
*Thunbergia alata
Tropaeolum

EVERGREEN CLIMBERS
(excluding the most tender conservatory climbers)

*Araujia sericofera
†*Asteranthera ovata*
†*Berberidopsis corallina*
Bignonia capreolata
†*Billardiera longiflora*
*Cissus
Clematis armandii
C. cirrhosa
Decumaria sinensis
†*Ercilla volubilis*
Euonymus fortunei var. *radicans*
*Ficus pumila
*Gelsemium sempervirens
*Hardenbergia violacea
Hedera
Holboellia
Hydrangea serratifolia
†*Jasminum mesnyi*
*J. polyanthum

†*Kadsura japonica*
*Lapageria rosea
*Lardizabala biternata
Lonicera (several)
†*Mitraria coccinea*
†*Mutisia*
†*Passiflora caerulea*
Pileostegia viburnoides
Rubus flagelliflorus
R. henryi
†*R. ichangensis*
R. lambertianus
*Semele androgyna
†*Senecio scandens*
*Smilax aspera
†*Sollya*
Stauntonia hexaphylla
†*Trachelospermum*

CLIMBERS WITH FRAGRANT FLOWERS

Actinidia arguta
A. deliciosa
A. kolomikta
A. polygama
Akebia quinata
*Anredera cordifolia
Apios tuberosa
*Araujia sericofera
*Beaumontia grandiflora
Clematis armandii
C. cirrhosa var. balearica
C. flammula
C. montana
†C. paniculata
C. rehderiana
Clematoclethra integrifolia
Decumaria sinensis
Holboellia latifolia
*Jasminum angulare
*J. azoricum
J. beesianum

J. officinale
*J. polyanthum
J. × stephanense
*J. simplicifolium subsp. suavissimum
*Lardizabala biternata
Lathyrus odoratus
Lonicera × americana
L. caprifolium
L. etrusca
L. × heckrotii
*L. hildebrandiana
L. japonica
L. periclymenum
*Mandevilla suaveolens
†*Pueraria lobata
Rosa (many)
Stauntonia hexaphylla
†Trachelospermum (all)
Vitis riparia
*Wattakaka sinensis
Wisteria (all)

ANNUAL AND BIENNIAL CLIMBERS
(or those that can be grown as such)

Adlumia fungosa
Clitoria mariana
Cobaea scandens
Cucurbita pepo
Eccremocarpus scaber
Humulus japonicus
Ipomoea
Lablab purpureus
Lathyrus (many)

Maurandia
Mina lobata
Oxypetalum coeruleum
Pueraria lobata
Rhodochiton atrosanguineum
Thladiantha dubia
Thunbergia alata
Tropaeolum majus

Glossary

aerial root A root originating above ground level.

anther Pollen-bearing part of the stamen.

axil Angle formed by a leaf or lateral branch with the stem.

berry Fleshy, usually several-seeded fruit.

bipinnate Twice pinnate.

bract Modified leaf at the base of a flower stalk or flower cluster.

calyx Collective term for the sepals of a flower.

capsule Dry fruit that splits to release its seeds.

clone A group of individuals derived originally from a single plant and maintained by vegetative propagation.

corolla Collective term for the petals of a flower.

corymb Flat-topped or rounded flowerhead with outer flowers opening first.

cultivar Garden variety, or a form found in the wild and maintained as a clone in cultivation.

cyme Flat-topped or rounded flowerhead with inner flowers opening first.

deciduous Seasonally falling – used of leaves.

dioecious Male and female flowers on different plants.

dissected Divided into many fine segments.

divided Separated to the base.

double Flowers with more than the usual number of petals and/or with style and stamens modified to petals.

entire Undivided, without teeth or lobes.

evergreen Remaining green throughout the winter.

family Group of genera with important characters in common, e.g. Rosaceae, rose family.

filament Stalk of the anther; together they form the stamen.

florets Small individual flowers of a dense inflorescence.

genus A group of species with important characters in common, e.g. *Rosa*, roses.

glaucous Covered with a blue-white or blue-grey bloom.

hermaphrodite Male or female flowers in the same inflorescence.

hybrid A cross between different species, subspecies or varieties.

inflorescence The flowering part of the plant.

leaflet The blade-like part of a compound leaf.

lobe Rounded, protruding part of a leaf, corolla or calyx.

monoecious Male and female flowers separate but on the same plant.

Opposite: *Clematis macropetela* (see page 69)

119

monotypic A genus having only one species.

node The point on a stem where the leaves arise.

palmate Lobed or divided like the fingers of a hand.

panicle An inflorescence with stalked flowers branching from a central stem.

pedicel Stalk of an individual flower in an inflorescence.

peduncle Stalk of a flower cluster or a single flower.

perfoliate Pair of opposite leaves joined at the base so they appear to surround the stem.

petal One of the parts of a corolla.

petiole Leaf stalk.

pinnate Leaflets arranged on either side of a central stalk (even pinnate: with an even number of leaflets, lacking a terminal leaflet; odd pinnate: with a terminal leaflet so the total number of leaflets is odd).

raceme Simple elongated inflorescence with stalked flowers, the lower opening first.

scandent With climbing stems.

sepal A division of a calyx outside the petals.

simple Describes leaves not compound, or inflorescences not branched.

species Basic unit of classification; a species is composed of similar but distinct individuals that interbreed freely among themselves, but not among

other species, e.g. *Rosa moschata*, the musk rose.

stamen The male organ of a flower.

staminode A sterile stamen, sometimes petal-like.

stigma The tip of the pistil, which receives the pollen.

stipule Appendage, often leafy (usually paired) at the base of some petioles.

subspecies Unit of classification below species, composed of individuals that differ from one another in minor characteristics, which are not sufficient to separate them as species, eg. *Clematis tibetana* subsp. *vernayi*.

tendril Twining or coiling thread-like structure formed from the whole or part of a stem, leaf or petiole.

tepal One of the segments of a flower in which petals and sepals are not differentiated.

trifoliate Three-leaved.

trifoliolate A compound leaf with three separate leaflets.

tuber Underground storage organ.

variety Unit of classification below species or subspecies, composed of individuals differing from the species in very minor characteristics.

vegetative propagation Method of increasing plants other than by seed, e.g. cuttings, layers.

Bibliography

Bean, W. J. *Trees and Shrubs Hardy in the British Isles* in four volumes, John Murray, 1970–1980.

Bean, W. J. *Wall Shrubs and Hardy Climbers* Putnam, 1939.

Beckett, Kenneth A. *Climbing Plants* Croom Helm, 1983.

Grey-Wilson, Christopher & Matthews, Victoria, *Gardening on Walls* Collins, 1983.

Hilliers' *Manual of Trees & Shrubs* David & Charles, 1972.

Lloyd, Christopher, *Clematis* Collins, 1977.

Thomas, Graham Stuart, *Climbing Roses Old & New* Dent, 1965.

Curtis's *Botanical Magazine* (now *The Kew Magazine*). This publication still maintains its long tradition of fine colour printing and articles on plants, plant collecting and conservation. Since it was established in 1787 nearly 10,500 colour plates have appeared by many of the best British botanical artists.

Acknowledgements

Line artwork by Dee Mclean, Linden Artists

Photographs

Pat Brindley, pages 23, 26, 27, 42, 58–9, 74, 81 (top), 86 (bottom), 87, 102, 103, 106; Linda Burgess, page 14; Crown copyright © reproduced with the permission of the Controller, Her Majesty's Stationery Office, and the Director, Royal Botanic Gardens, Kew, pages 6, 10, 84, 89, 92; John Glover, pages 18, 67, 79, 91 (top); Photos Horticultural, pages 31, 34, 35, 43, 50, 54, 55, 66, 70 (bottom), 71, 75, 81 (bottom), 83, 90, 99, 107 (bottom), 114, 118; Brian Mathew, pages 47, 63 (bottom), 107 (top), 110; S. & O. Mathews, page 19; Jane Taylor, page 86 (top); John Simmons, pages 63 (top), 91 (bottom); The Harry Smith Horticultural Photographic Collection, pages 30, 39, 62, 70 (top), 78 (top and bottom), 94 (top and bottom), 95, 98, 111.

Pictures on pages 76, 80, 104, 109 are reproduced with the permission of The Royal Botanic Gardens, Kew.
Bougainvillea glabra on page 64 © The Botany Directorate of the Ministry of Agriculture and Agrarian Reform, Baghdad.

Taxonomy checked by Susyn Andrews, who works as a botanist at The Royal Botanic Gardens, Kew, and is also a member of The Kew Magazine Editorial Committee. She studied amenity horticulture at The National Botanic Gardens, Glasnevin, Co. Dublin, Republic of Ireland.

Index